Mammals
of the North Woods

By Roger & Consie Powell

Kollath+Stensaas
PUBLISHING

To

Odin, Freja, Loki, Leweasel, ThaCho,

Uskool, Gherkin, Lucinda, Bessie, Kim,

Carlo, Sylvia, Raja and Sammy

Kollath+Stensaas Publishing
394 Lake Avenue South, Suite 406
Duluth, MN 55802
Office: 218.727.1731
Orders: 800.678.7006
info@kollathstensaas.com
www.kollathstensaas.com

MAMMALS *of the* NORTH WOODS

Printed in South Korea by Doosan
10 9 8 7 6 5 4 3 2 1   First Edition

Editorial Director: Mark Sparky Stensaas
Graphic Designer: Rick Kollath

ISBN 13: 978-1-936571-09-3

Table of Contents

WHAT IS A MAMMAL?

Mammals are truly amazing.

Mammals make the world's best food for their kids. A female mammal makes food that is designed to meet her offspring's needs perfectly, she makes it herself. She does not have to find bugs to shove down throats. Nope. She makes milk, amazing milk.

Mammals protect their developing babies. A female mammal protects her developing offspring in her uterus, providing the food they need, protecting them from predators. She need not worry about a predator stealing her eggs from a nest. Pregnancy is absolutely amazing.

Mammals have hair. Hair keeps them warm, protects them from the sun and rain, and allows them to hide or to be bold and obvious. It is amazing.

Mammals have fancy teeth. They have teeth that come in four different styles with fancy shapes that do different jobs. Youngsters have special expendable teeth. Teeth are amazing.

Mammals have cool ways to perceive their worlds. Most mammals have the standard 5 senses: vision, hearing, smell, touch, taste; what they do with those senses is often amazing. Some mammals even have additional senses.

Mammals are smart. Being smart allows mammals to have flexible behaviors. They can learn quickly. They can fit their behavior to each situation. That is amazing.

Mammals have special skills. Some mammals run fast, some dig deep holes, some are expert swimmers, some fly. Look at all mammals and you can find one or more that can go about just anywhere, getting there in about any manner, to do just about anything once it gets there.

Yep, mammals are amazing. We are mammals.

For mammalogists, the people who study mammals and how they evolved, mammals are defined by their jaw joint. Every mammal has only one bone on each side of the lower jaw and that bone hinges to the squamosal bones in the skull to make the jaw joint. The reptiles from which mammals evolved had several bones in their lower jaws, some of which have become parts of the inner ears of mammals, and had different bones making the jaw hinge. The simple yet strong jaw has been advantageous for mammals through their evolution. For most people, however, mammals are defined by producing milk and by having hair.

lk

female mammals produce milk in mammary glands to feed to their born young. The milk of different mammal species differs because mammals of different species have different needs. The composition milk changes over time, matching the changing needs of youngsters they grow.

centa

female mammals in the North Woods, except possums, cooperate biologically and developmentally with their unborn offspring, and tically with their mates, to build a complex placenta, a life support em that is like no other. A placenta transports from a mother mam- to a growing fetus within her uterus all the nutrition that the fetus ds. The placenta even transports chemicals from the mother's food, hing the fetus what foods will be safe and nutritious after it is born. placenta transports the waste products of life and growth back to mother to process. Life in the uterus introduces a fetus to the world hich its mother lives while keeping the fetus safe and warm and well This is quite the life support system.

ir

cally, all mammals have hair, to some degree. Most mammals have kinds of hair: long, stiff guard hairs and soft underfur. Guard hairs e in many colors from white through shades of brown, red and gray, lack. Guard hairs lay flat all around a mammal, providing a protec- coat that keeps the mammal from being scraped and scratched by ches and rocks. Its color can help a mammal blend into its environ- t and make it hard for a predator to see. Some mammals use special rs, such as the white patch under a white-tailed deer's tail to com- icate with other members of their species. The guard hairs of still r mammals make them stand out and be obvious, like the black and te stripes of skunks that warn other critters to stay away. Some mam- s even have guard hairs that protect them from predators: porcupines' ls are modified guard hairs. Guard hairs have a thin coat of oil that ls water and keeps the underfur dry and functional in the rain and when swimming.

underfur lies below the guard hairs and provides insulation against eme temperatures. Underfur is usually light gray and is soft as down, use it functions the same way as a bird's down feathers, to keep its nal warm.

st mammals shed their hair and produce a new coat once each year, lly in spring or summer. By the end of winter, guard hairs have been

battered for a year and many are tattered at their tips. In some mamm
the shedding and regrowth of new hair can take months, leaving t
with a thin coat in summer. By autumn, underfur has regrown and
new guard hairs are full grown. Some mammals, however, shed and
duce new coats twice a year. Weasels and snowshoe hares grow br
coats for the summer and white coats for the winter, making their
coats obvious. For the other mammals that shed twice a year, the
coats are similar in color and not so obvious.

Teeth

A mammal's teeth are important tools that help it live and grow
mammal's teeth also show us what the mammal eats and how old
Predatory mammals have certain types of pointy teeth. Mammals tha
plants only have teeth with ridges for shredding plants. Mammals
have general diets or eat nuts have blunt teeth. And, as mammals g
older, first they lose their baby (or deciduous) teeth and grow adul
permanent) teeth. Then, as they grow older yet, their teeth wear dow

Mammal teeth are coated with enamel, the strongest material n
by any animals. Teeth come in 4 different styles that do different j
Incisor teeth are in the front of a mammal's mouth and most mamm
use their incisors to manipulate food. Incisors, as well as other typ
teeth, vary in number across mammal species, so mammalogists use a
mula for describing teeth, counting the number of teeth in each quad
of the mouth (upper jaw right side, upper jaw left side, lower jaw r
side, and lower jaw left side). Every rodent has 1 big incisor tooth in
quadrant, adding up to the 4 big, obvious teeth we associate with rode
Deer have no upper incisors at all but each has 3 lower incisors on
side of the jaw. A wolf has 3 small incisor teeth in each quadrant. C
marsupials have more than 3 incisors; our possums here in the N
Woods have 5 in each upper quadrant and 4 in each lower quadrant

Canine teeth come behind the incisors and no mammal has more th
in each quadrant of its mouth. Predatory mammals use their canine
grab and kill prey. Lower canines of deer look like, and are snuggled
to, their lower incisors. Rodents have no canine teeth.

Right after the canine teeth come premolars. Deciduous premolars
shaped like the adult molars; deciduous teeth do not include mo
Adult premolars are often shaped similarly to molars but are usu
smaller and simpler than molars. Together, premolars and molars
called cheek teeth and they are the most complicated of mamma
teeth. Human cheek teeth and those of bears have rounded cusps and
used mostly for crushing and grinding. The cheek teeth of rodents

bits and deer have complex ridges that serve to rip plant material into bits. The cheek teeth of shrews, moles and bats are pointy to crunch grind dead insects. And the cheek teeth of predatory mammals ude unique, self-sharpening teeth, called carnassial teeth, that these mmals use to slice flesh. When premolars and molars have similar bes, telling them apart is nearly impossible.

nifty formula that describes a mammal's teeth pattern shows the abers of teeth of each type on one side of the mouth. The figure on e 35 shows how dental formulae work.

ses

general, all mammals have the standard five senses that we humans e: sight, sound, smell, taste and touch. Most mammals have other es, too. Consider whiskers. Some people might consider what whis-do to be a type of touch but whiskers are so much fancier. Not only whiskers feel solid objects that a mammal might not see in the dark, skers can feel air currents, telling mammals of movements by other nals nearby. Otters probably use their whiskers to follow turbulence s made by fish in cloudy water. Whiskers are officially called vibrissae.

s and shrews use echolation. Star-nosed moles detect electric currents n their nose tentacles. Vampire bats (which do not live in the North ods) can sense infrared radiation. Undoubtedly, other mammals have es we do not yet know.

netheless, most mammals live in a world of smells. Have you ever adered what your dog smells at a fire hydrant? Very likely, he smells Joe (the dog next door) has visited the hydrant very recently but ry has not been here since yesterday; Susan is coming into heat portant for boy dogs to remember); Jane has just gone out of heat get her for 6 months); and 3 new dogs have stopped in the past day: boy who thinks he's pretty hot stuff, another boy who smells submis-, and a young gal who is still growing up. Your dog learns things; he is simply sniffing the hydrant. The hydrant is the dogs' social medium. at smell communicates is powerful.

mmals use smell to find food, to avoid becoming food for someone , to keep track of their environments and to know where they are, and eep track of members of their own species in both a general and a per-al sort of way. In the smell department, we humans have been gypped.

narts

ally, mammals are smart. Mammals' large brains allow them to learn ckly, to remember, and to discover new things. Every mammal has a period of family life during which it interacts daily with its mother. T[...] social group of mother and young is the foundation for all variants [...] social life for mammals. Many mammals live in social groups as adu[...] For many, that social group starts with the family core and then a[...] older siblings and sometimes a father. Wolves and beavers, for examp[...] live in just such extended family groups with parents and siblings b[...] in recent years. White-tailed deer live in matriarchal groups of a mot[...] and her daughters of recent years, often including granddaughters a[...] aunts. When matriarchal groups coalesce they become herds. Someti[...] males join the herds. Being smart allows mammals keep track of w[...] happens in their social groups.

In contrast to "social" mammals, the family core for most mam[...] species breaks up when offspring are able to fend for themselves. Th[...] mammals that appear to live their lives alone are sometimes called "s[...] tary" mammals, yet no mammal is truly solitary. None can afford [...] ignore what neighbors of their own species are doing. Neighbors mi[...] eat food a given mammal wants to eat, or alert prey to become w[...] and hard to catch. Keeping track of neighbors is important and, the[...] fore, the so-called "solitary" mammals communicate using scent ma[...] from diverse glands: glands associated with urinating and defecating[...] well as glands on feet and backs and chins and ankles. Remember y[...] dog and the fire hydrant. All mammals keep track of their neighb[...] whether they live with them daily or not. Being smart allows mamm[...] to do this.

Every adult mammal that is a resident of a particular place has a ho[...] range: that area of ground where it knows the locations of food and s[...] sleeping sites, the escape routes from predators, and who its neighb[...] are and what they normally do. A home range contains all the resour[...] an individual mammal needs to live and to reproduce. If an individu[...] home range contains more resources than it needs, it might share all [...] parts of that home range with other members of its species. If the ho[...] range contains just enough to support one individual, then it is n[...] shared and the home range is called a territory.

Every species of mammal has a single scientific name, like *Canis lu[...]* for the wolf and *Castor canadensis* for the beaver. In contrast, no ma[...] mals have official common names. Consequently, some people c[...] members of the species *Bison bison* buffalo and other people call the[...] bison. Both names are equally correct. In this guide, we include m[...] tiple common names for species that have them.

LASSIFICATION OF MAMMALS

ithin the classification of animals, Mammalia is a Class within the Phylum Chordata (the animals with notochords, a hollow nerve rd) and within the subphylum Vertebrata (the animals with verte-e, or back bones). Within Mammalia, species are divided into Orders t constitute major evolutionary lineages, such as Carnivora, the meat ers, and Rodentia, the rodents. Most species in an order have many racteristics in common with other species in the order. Thus, all spe-in the Carnivora have carnassial teeth or evolved from ancestors who them, and all species in the Rodentia have ONE large incisor in each drant of the mouth. The names for all Orders of animals end in "a." cies are further grouped into Families, which are evolutionary lineages hin Orders. All species in the Family Canidae are closely related to nestic dogs while all species with the Family Felidae are closely related lomestic cats. The names for Families of animals end in "dae." Within h Family, species are listed by their scientific names, which include a us name and a species name. Thus, *Canis lupus* is the scientific name the wolf species and *Canis latrans* is for the coyote species. Both of se species are classified within the Genus *Canis*, which constitutes the species that are most closely related to the domestic dog, *Canis iliaris*. The wolf and coyote species are distinguished as unique species hin the Genus *Canis* by having different species names.

ctly speaking, a "species" is a *category of classification* and *not* a living, athing, furry critter. A species is a human concept used to organize in minds the animals we see in the woods. Thus, a species can not hunt ee hunted because it is only an concept in our minds. Members of a cies, however, are real animals and they do eat and sleep and they do t or be hunted.

MAMMAL TRACK & SIGN

People interested in mammals spend their lives looking down, in contrast to bird watchers, who spend their lives looking up. Most mammals are secretive and avoid humans. Consequently, mammal watchers spend a lot of time looking down for tracks, scats (feces) and other signs that mammals leave.

Tracks

Counting toes on tracks tells a lot about who left a track and how the mammal lives. The standard issue for toes on mammals is 5: a thumb or big toe on each paw and 4 more fingers. Some mammals, however, have fewer toes, especially mammals that run. Canids (members of the dog family, the Canidae) and felids (members of the cat family, the Felidae) have 4 toes that reach the ground on each foot. The first digit on each foot (the thumb or big toe) is either missing or tiny and not long enough to reach the ground. Having one fewer toe on each foot makes the foot lighter and easier to lift and lift and lift when running. Deer have 3 feet toes that reach the ground on each foot. Just their 3rd and 4th digits touch the ground, each covered with an elaborate claw called a hoof. Their feet are lighter yet and easier to lift.

For example, if you look at a track in the mud or snow and count only 2 toes covered by hooves, you know that a white-tailed deer, a moose, a wapiti, or a caribou left the track. Moose, wapiti and caribou have restricted ranges in the North Woods so, depending on where you are, you can narrow your options for who left the track.

Tracks of a moose can be over 6 inches long. Look for them near wet areas in summer.

Tracks of white-tailed deer are the smallest (around 3 inches long), caribou and wapiti tracks larger (4 inches or a bit larger), and moose tracks huge (6 inches and more).

The 4 toes showing in canid tracks have 4 toes and their claws show most of the time. Canid tracks also grade in size, as tracks of the different

r do. Wolf tracks are largest, then coyote, then red fox, then gray fox
cks. Tracks of wild canids tend to be somewhat elongate, especially the
d paw tracks, in contrast to the tracks of dogs, which are more round,
cat tracks. Bobcat and lynx tracks have 4 toes each, like canid tracks,
usually do not show the claws.

cks of black bears are big; hind foot tracks look modestly like those of
are-foot person, and all feet have 5 toes, all showing prominent claws
oto pg. 86). Raccoons have much smaller tracks also with 5 toes that
w claws, but the toes are relatively long and skinny (photo pg. 82).

ats

mmals also leave scats, which also provide a mammal-watcher with
ormation. Predatory mammals, the carnivores, often leave scats on
ds, especially unpaved roads. Roads make for easy travel and a preda-
that wants to travel some distance often walks along a road going its
. Carnivore scats are usually elongate and may have hair, bone chips,
fruit seeds identifiable on the surface. Unfortunately, most carnivore

scats are hard to differentiate
to species. Black bears' scats
are sometimes so big that
no other animal could have
left them. Bear cubs' scats,
however, are often small and
no bigger than a raccoon's
or gray fox's scat. Bear scats
are likely to have fruit seeds
visible on their surfaces but
raccoons and gray foxes also
eat lots of fruit in summer.
Thus, overlaps of scat sizes
and animal diets make deter-
mining who left a scat an
imperfect science.

scat of a wolf is large and full of hair and bones.
helps distinguish it from dog feces.

In the past, some naturalists took pride in being able
to identify scats to species.
ent research using DNA techniques to identify scats has shown
t those naturalists were not as good at scat identification as they had
ught they were. Most field guides to mammal tracks include drawings
photos of scats and you can use these to help you become as good as
one else at identifying scats.

Skulls

If you find a mammal skull, look at the teeth and check the de
formula, or as much of the dental formula as you can figure out fr
what is left of the skull (see page 35 for a table of the dental formulae

all North Woods mammals).
Size of the skull and teeth
can get you a long ways
towards being able to identify a skull. The skull also
provides other information
about its owner. Whether
the skull has deciduous or
permanent teeth tells you
whether the mammal died as
a youngster or adult. If the
teeth are worn and if teeth
are missing and their sockets

**Skulls can tell us much about the living animal. Ch
the teeth and compare to the dental formula.**

grown over with bone tells you that the mammal was very old whe
died. Small rodents eat skulls and antlers they find to get calcium. If
see small tooth marks on a skull, it has been in the woods for a while

Other Signs

Mammal watchers do not have to
spend their whole lives looking down
at their feet, though. Herbivorous
mammals often leave sign of their
winter dining on the branches of saplings and shrubs. Because white-tailed
deer and moose lack upper incisors,
they do not slice plants. Instead, a
deer or moose takes hold of a small
branch by pushing it against its upper
gum with its lower incisors and then
rips the branch off. During summer,
one can still see those jagged, ripped
ends of branches. Rabbits, hares and

**Beaver chewed tree. Finding animal sig
can be very rewarding.**

rodents do slice the plants they eat, leaving cleanly cut ends to brancl
These mammals often girdle trees and shrubs in winter. They seek
inner, living bark of the plants, called cambium. And beavers le
stumps, of course, showing where they have cut trees.

Many good books about mammal tracks and sign are available.

TUDYING MAMMALS
N THE FIELD

esearchers who study mammals in the field spend a lot of time both
looking down and looking around and up. New research tools keep
oming available and field mammalogists are quick to adopt new tools,
le continuing to use the old standbys.

en possible, researchers still observe mammals directly. Many mam-
s can be habituated to being watched by people, especially squirrels
also deer and even carnivores. Red foxes can be observed at their
s from a distance in spring and summer by a person with patience,
istence and a calm demeanor. Diverse, remotely triggered cameras
now available, too, that can be set across a landscape to photograph
nmals. Every mammal differs from all others, even those like deer
e and red squirrels who all seem identical, but some have individually
ntifiable marks so obvious that people can see them readily. Cameras
w the field mammalogist to document the diversity of medium-sized
arge mammals in an area and sometimes even to estimate the num-
s of individuals. Track plates can be set using diverse tunnel systems,
wing identification of species and sometimes individual mammals.
h tunnels outfitted with something that catches hair, or barbed wire
ing bait for bears, and other methods of catching hair provide bits of

ail camera can really open your eyes to what critters are living in your area. Black bear on
I day, coyote at a deer carcass and a bobcat, an animal rarely seen in the day.

skin that laboratory-types can use to identify species and individuals analyzing DNA.

When more information is needed, especially for mammals that are se tive, field mammalogists live-trap. Live-trapping medium-sized to l mammals requires special training, skill, and permits to use immobiliz drugs. Handling small mammals often does not require immobiliz drugs but, nonetheless, requires training. Live-trapped mammals be measured, blood and other tissue samples can be collected safely understand individual and population health, and the animals can outfitted with telemetry equipment. Telemetry has matured over past five decades. In the 1960s, telemetry collars transmitted beeps were received by radios that mammalogists and other biologists car by hand into the field. Now, even very small mammals can be outfi with collars bearing global positioning system (GPS) equipment other satellite communications allowing the collars to track themsel Accelerometers and video cameras mounted on collars, hormones lected from scats, metabolic rates measured using doubly-labelled w and more tools and techniques can now be used to study wild mamr right where they live.

AMMAL ORDERS & FAMILIES

der Didelphimorphia
sum-like mammals

mily Didelphidae
w World Possums — Virginia opossum

supials constitute a major group of mammals that are most common
ustralia and South America. Our Virginia opossum is the only mar-
al species in North America but other possums live in Central and
th America. Marsupials differ from so-called "placental" mammals by
ng reproductive systems that have rudimentary placentas able to sup-
embryos for only very short gestation periods. These reproductive
ems also emphasize lactation as the major support for young. Some
ale marsupials (but not our opossums) are able to nurse two young
ifferent ages on different teats, with each teat supplying milk of a
position tuned to the age of the youngster attached to it.

possumlike marsupials in the Americas have general, stocky body
ds, 5 toes on each paw, and opposable big toes. They are all good
bers but also forage on the ground. They have mostly naked, prehen-
tails. Their senses of smell and hearing are excellent but their vision
ot as outstanding. Their eyes are situated part way down the sides of
r faces, giving them modest binocular vision looking forward but also
onable vision to the sides to watch for predators.

group, marsupials often have more teeth than "placental" mammals.
maximum number of teeth for "placental" mammals is 44; possum
50 teeth. It is no wonder that, when a possum hisses and opens its
in threat, it appears to have a mouth full of teeth—it does. The cheek
h of possums have lots of sharp cusps, which are good for crunching
rtebrates.

der Carnivora
datory Mammals

Order of mammals called the Carnivora includes the mammals who
ain (or whose ancestors obtained) a significant portion of their nutri-
by killing and eating other vertebrates. "Carnivore" means meat
r. These mammals are called carnivores because they are members
he Carnivora but also because of their predatory, carnivorous habits.

Nonetheless, the name can be confusing because mammals of s[...] other orders, such as the frog-eating bats, are also highly carnivo[...] even though they are not members of the Carnivora and are not ca[...] carnivores.

All of the species that are members of the Carnivora are characterize[...] having (or having evolved from a species that had) a special pair of t[...] on each side of the jaw. These are the carnassial teeth and actually co[...] tute the last upper premolar and the first lower molar on each side. T[...] teeth are particularly fancy because they are sharp, for slicing flesh, [...] they are self sharpening. The carnassials are big teeth positioned abou[...] to ¾ of the way back in the jaw and each has 2 points with a V-sha[...] notch between them. The upper carnassial on each side lies outside [...] lower one when they meet as the jaw is closed, and the notches lin[...] when the jaw closes. The result is that when meat muscle or tend[...] lined up in the valleys of the teeth, the teeth pull together as they c[...] both slicing the meat on their sharp edges and rubbing the teeth ag[...] each other, keeping the edges sharp.

All members of the dog, cat and weasel families (except otters) have [...] developed carnassials and prey on other vertebrates for most of their d[...] Though the ancestors of bears did have carnassials, living bears do [...] Instead, their back premolars and their molars have rounded cusps [...] they use the teeth for crushing.

Carnivore species fall into two groups, the dog group, sometimes ca[...] the canoids, and the cat group, sometimes called feloids. The dog gr[...] is more diverse, containing the dog, weasel, skunk, bear and racc[...] families as well as the seals and sea lions. The cat group includes the [...] hyaena, mongoose, civet and malagasy carnivore families.

As a group, carnivores are smart and able to learn new foods and [...] to procure them. Some, like wolves and some coyotes, live in exten[...] family groups and have complex social behaviors for living in gro[...] Many others forage singly but, nonetheless, maintain social contact v[...] all their neighbors using a web of olfactory, auditory and visual c[...] munications.

Family Canidae

Dogs — wolf, coyote, red fox, gray fox

Members of the dog family, the canids, resemble dogs, having faces v[...] distinct muzzles and pointed ears, and standing tall on legs that are ab[...] as long as their backs. Most have long, bushy tails, often with a contr[...]

color at the tip. They are all, except perhaps for gray foxes, familiar
most people who have an interest in the out-of-doors.

d canids live on all continents except Antarctica but, even there, dogs
ed people to explore the continent and hauled people to the South
. The canid species fall into two major groups, the wolf-like canids
the fox-like canids. Across North America we have a confusing diver-
of wolf-like canids that includes wolves, eastern wolves, red wolves,
tes and various possible hybrids of these canids. We also have red
s, Arctic foxes, gray foxes and several smaller foxes. Fox-like canids
distinctive for the modestly skunk-like smell of the mercaptans (sul-
r compounds) in their urine. Wolves, Ethiopian wolves, jackals, some
r wolf-like canids, and red foxes and some other fox species live in
sia and Africa. A number of fox species live in South America and
foxes have been introduced to Australia.

r species of the dog family live in the North Woods, not counting
estic dogs themselves: wolf, coyote, red fox and gray fox. All are com-
at least in some areas.

ids' legs are adapted for running, especially for long distances. Their
are long and their feet, even the relatively large feet of wolves, are
pact with only 4 toes that meet the ground, not the standard 5 for
mals. Wolves can trot for dozens of miles.

ids live in a world alive with sensual input. All have good binocular
n, which helps them find and chase prey. Their hearing is highly
d and their long muzzles provide room for an exceptional sense of
l. Coyotes and foxes use their large ears for hearing prey in deep grass
under snow.

anids scent mark to communicate the extent of their home ranges to
r members of their species. Dominant males of all species lift their
and urinate to scent mark as well as to send a visual signal of domi-
e. Squatting to urinate or to defecate also leaves a scent mark, as does
ching, with hind feet especially, after defecating. Canids have glands
eir feet that leave scent when they scratch the ground.

f our canids have 42 teeth (see pg. 35 for dental formulae of all North
ds mammals). All premolars are pointed and the carnassial teeth are
developed; all canids use their carnassial teeth for slicing flesh as they
The molars behind their carnassials, however, have flattened surfaces
rinding and crushing. Canids use these molars for eating fruits and
sionally grains. Wolves' and coyotes' scats are often filled with rasp-
y seeds in August.

t males and females of all canid species maintain long-term pair

bonds that form the centers of their year-round social groups. Wo[lves]
live predominantly in packs, which are extended family groups wi[th a]
pair of parents and their young from the past few years. Coyotes in m[any]
populations, and red foxes in a few, also live in packs. Gray foxes, h[ow]ever, appear never to live in extended family groups, though parents [may]
forage together outside the reproductive season.

All four of our canids can live in habitats that range from deep fores[t to]
prairies and open farm fields. All but wolves, perhaps, appear to th[rive]
in a mix of habitats with open country punctuated by scattered to l[arge]
patches of forest.

The size gradation from wolves, which are big, through coyotes to [red]
foxes and then gray foxes, which are the smallest, often affects wh[ich]
canids live in a particular area. Down their relative size gradient, m[em]-bers of each species compete most with canids of the species adjacen[t in]
size. This competition leads canids to prey on members of the next sm[all]-er species. Consequently, red foxes often having healthier populat[ions]
where they co-exist with wolves than where they co-exist with coyote[s.]

Dogs have been domesticated from wolves that co-existed with hum[ans]
tens of thousands of years ago. Because of this relationship, dogs s[hare]
many behaviors with wolves. Domestic dogs, though, are not sim[ply]
wolves that live with people. During the process of domestication, [dogs]
may have domesticated humans and themselves as much as hum[ans]
domesticated dogs. Dogs use the social behaviors they inherited f[rom]
wolves to facilitate their living together with people. The result is [that]
dogs and humans can communicate to each other and can cooperat[e to]
complete joint tasks. No other pair of species cooperates the way [dogs]
and people do. Dogs *are* special.

Not all domestic dogs live with people, however, and domestic dogs [that]
do live with people often wander on their own. Some free-ranging [dogs]
learn to kill domestic livestock and to hunt deer but most dogs you m[ight]
meet in the woods are simply on a jaunt. Dogs' tracks tend to be a[bit]
rounder than the tracks of wild canids and, because dogs vary great[ly in]
size, some dog tracks overlap in size with the tracks of all the wild ca[nids.]

Family Mephitidae

Skunks — skunks & stink badgers

Skunks live only in North America and the stink badgers live onl[y in]
southeast Asia. The 6 species of skunks are striped skunks, hoo[ded]
skunks, two species of hognosed skunks, and eastern and western sp[otted]

ks. Here in the North woods, we enjoy striped skunks but rarely get
e eastern spotted skunks.

skunks and stink badgers defend themselves by expelling noxious
nicals. Their highly evolved anal glands produce large amounts of
captans (sulphur compounds) and the associated muscles can spray
e compounds with accurate aim up to two yards or farther. The spray
cause temporary blindness and nausea in humans and other mam-
if received in heavy doses. The recipe of compounds in skunks' and
k badgers' anal glands presumably differ among individuals. Skunks
stink badgers also use their anal gland excretions for scent marking.

ks' anal glands are not inexhaustible, so skunks are not overly
r to blast other critters or people unless necessary. A skunk warns
tential target first with foot stamping and teeth chattering. These
ings are followed by raising the tail and changing posture. Most
ks bend their bodies into a U-shape but spotted skunks can spray
a handstand. Once the aiming posture is reached, a blast usually
ws. Abbreviated warning rituals precede a surprise encounter, so do
depend on a full warning. Mostly, however, skunks prefer to co-exist
other animals in peace.

he skunks have generalized mammalian skeletons with no special
tations for locomotion. They have the standard issue of 5 toes on
foot. Skunks' heads are triangular with modest muzzles. Their eyes
laced to provide binocular vision. Their senses of hearing and smell
excellent.

striped and spotted skunks have 34 teeth. Hognosed skunks have
fewer upper premolar on each side. All premolars are pointed and
carnassial teeth are well developed. The rear molars, however, have
ened surfaces for crushing and grinding fruits, seeds and insects.

nily Mustelidae

sels — weasels, mink, martens, fisher, ferrets, badger, otter

weasel family, the mustelids, is more diverse than any other family
arnivores in the North Woods. They comprise three weasel species
t weasel, short-tailed weasel, long-tailed weasel), mink, fisher, mar-
otter, badger and an occasional wolverine. Mustelids are, in general,
ively long with short legs, setting them close to the ground. The
els, mink and otter are most extreme but even a wolverine, the larg-
f the group, shows its distinctive skinniness and short legs when in
mer coat.

Across the globe, the weasel family is more diverse yet. Wild populat[ions] live in Eurasia, Africa, the Americas and 3 species have been introdu[ced] to New Zealand. Eurasia has a number of small weasel species and 7 [spe-] cies of martens, some of which live in tropical areas. Three ferret spe[cies] parcel out Europe and western Asia, the rest of Asia, and the Great Pl[ains] of North America. South America and Africa support more species y[et.]

Their long bodies and short legs lead mustelids to run with a distinc[t] gait. A weasel's front paws touch the ground with one slightly in fron[t of] the other. As the weasel pushes off with front paws, it hunches its b[ack] so that its hind paws fall right into the track left by the front paws. [The] result is a track pattern with well-spaced pairs of paw prints, one slig[htly] ahead of the other.

Martens, fishers and wolverines have 38 teeth and the same dental form[ula.] All premolars are pointed and the carnassial teeth are well develo[ped.] Weasels and badgers have 3 premolars top and bottom, while otters ha[ve 4] top and 3 bottom. Otters' cheek teeth have rounded cusps, much like o[urs.]

All mustelids are predominantly predatory, preying on small to medi[um-] sized mammals and on birds and eggs. Some will eat fruits during mid[to] late summer but the members of the three weasel species are as extr[eme] predators as the cats, which seldom eat any vegetation at all. The wea[sels'] teeth show their extreme predatory habitats, having no really functi[onal] teeth for grinding behind their carnassials.

In all mustelid species, males can grow to be considerably larger t[han] females. The largest male fisher we have handled weighed abou[t 12] pounds but the largest female weighed less than 6 pounds. Males c[om-] pete with each other, and fight, during the breeding season to gain ac[cess] to females. Big males probably father most kits. Females, however, h[ave] sole responsibility for raising young. Besides the energy costs of lactat[ion,] females must catch enough food to feed the whole family once yo[ung] start eating solid food. The result is that females raising young expen[d as] much energy in a day as do big males.

Female mustelids of most species delay implantation of their fetuses; [this] occurs when the fetuses reach the blastocyst stage, the developme[ntal] stage during which fetuses implant in the uterine wall. The blasto[cysts] go dormant within the uterus and, for some species, stay dormant fo[r up] to 10 months. During this period of delay, detecting whether a fe[male] is pregnant is impossible. Implantation is triggered by changing [day] length in spring and once blastocysts implant, a normal gestation foll[ows.] Inserting a developmental delay into the reproductive cycle is hypothes[ized] to have evolved only in species for which the optimum time for gi[ving] birth comes longer after mating than the normal time taken for gestat[ion.]

populations of weasels, minks, fishers and martens, males that grow mature with abundant food can grow to be very big. Males that growing food shortage never grow to be as big. Thus, the average degree exual dimorphism of body size in a population changes through time across each species' range.

ers often live in family groups but all other mustelids live and forage e, except when mothers are raising kits. Most maintain territories they do not share with other members of their own sex and species. territories of males and females, however, overlap.

mily Procyonidae

ccoons — raccoon, coatis, ringtails, kinkajous

raccoon family is relatively small with only about 10 member spe-. Raccoons are the only representatives in the North Woods. Ringtails white-nosed coatis reside in the southwestern United States and her south. Kinkajous and other procyonids live in Central and South erica.

cyonids have generalized body builds, making them good at climbing s but letting them forage and travel on the ground as well. All have 5 on each foot. The cheek teeth have rounded cusps for crushing and hassials are not well developed.

st procyonids are predominantly nocturnal and have relatively large that face forward, giving them good binocular vision. Their senses of ll and hearing are also good. They are all omnivorous to frugivorous ing mainly fruit).

mily Ursidae

ars — black bear, brown bear, polar bear, giant panda

rs are large-bodied, stocky mammals with broad heads, short tails, ng limbs and 5 toes on each foot. Of the 8 species, 6 bear species live urasia, 1 lives in South America, 3 live in North America (brown s, polar bears and black bears) and only one, the North American k bear, lives in the North Woods.

ar bears are white, giant pandas are contrasting black and white, the rest of the bears are variations on black to brown, most with chest patches and other markings. Both polar bears and pandas are que in other ways. Polar bears live in the Arctic and are almost entirely ivorous, specializing on seals. Giant pandas have a constricted range

in the mountains of China and are herbivorous specialists on bamb
The other bears are mostly omnivorous, though brown bears, of
called grizzly bears in North America, can be predominantly carnivor
at times. Black bears have 42 teeth. All the cheek teeth except the
premolars, which are just tiny stubs of teeth, are flattened with mult
cusps for grinding.

Except for mothers with cubs, bears live alone. They communicate w
other bears from a distance by scent marking. When bears meet, they
a language of facial expressions and vocalizations. Bears have excell
senses of smell and hearing, making vision their least important of th
three senses.

Most bears' lives are dominated by the annual disappearance of almos
food at a predictable time each year. Before that time, bears eat mas
amounts of food to put on enough fat to support them during a l
fast. For polar bears, that fast time comes when Arctic sea ice breaks
in summer, making seals difficult to impossible to hunt. For black
brown bears, the time comes at the beginning of winter when ber
nuts and social insects are gone. These bears then enter a 5 to 7 mo
period of what we call winter lethargy. Most bears enter dens, wh
may be holes under root masses, small caves or even a nest on the gro
where they can become covered with snow. During winter lethargy, b
do not eat, drink, urinate or defecate, yet their body temperatures do
fall but a few degrees and their metabolic rates decrease only mode
Bears spend the period of lethargy dozing but they are capable of r
ning if disturbed. We have never looked into a bear's winter den with
seeing the bear looking out at us. Come spring, the challenge of gai
weight to survive the next winter starts all over again.

Bears' home ranges may be as small as 5 square miles for a female N
American black bear living where food is abundant. They can be as l
as hundreds of square miles for brown and black bears where foo
scarce. Polar bears' home ranges are thousands of square miles.

Female bears delay implantation during gestation, as do most muste
(see the section on the Mustelidae). North American black bears
brown bears breed during summer but give birth to tiny cubs in c
during mid-winter. Cubs nurse through the winter and by early sp
have grown to what would be considered an average birth size for o
mammals as big as bears.

nily Felidae

s — bobcat, lynx, puma, lion, tigers, jaguars, leopards

)pecies of cats are recognizable as cats, resembling domestic cats to
e degree. Most have rounded faces with eyes aimed forward, and
ited ears, some with tufts. Most cats have long tails. Many cats have
ted coats, which have made their pelts valuable in the fur trade and
led to some species being endangered. Over 35 species of cats exist
.nd the world, inhabiting all continents except Antarctica, if we count
feral domestic cats in Australia. Most wild cats are relatively small,
size of bobcats and smaller, but a distinct group of species are big:
, tiger, jaguar, leopard and a few others. We have three species of
cats in the North Woods, none of which is considered big. We also
 feral domestic cats, which are common across the southern part of
egion. Bobcats are resident and widespread, lynxes are resident north
ie Great Lakes, and pumas (or mountain lions) are regular, though
)mmon, visitors.

:ats are built on the same basic body plan. Cats have rounded feet
 four toes touching the ground on each paw, instead of the standard
 of five toes for mammals. The reduced number of toes means that
are good runners. Cats' feet are relatively bigger than those of canids
all but cheetahs have retractable claws, which are sharp and can be
nded to hold prey. In addition, cats' legs are generally stockier and
e muscular than those of canids. Thus, cats are best at sprinting and
iot able to trot the long distances that canids can. Cats have good,
icular vision and excellent hearing and smell. With short faces and
ller area inside the muzzle for sensing smells, cats emphasize vision
ewhat more and smell somewhat less than do canids.

 cats, along with some of the weasels, are the most carnivorous of all
imals. Many obtain all of their nutrition from eating vertebrate prey
 most have reduced numbers of cheek teeth, not needing teeth for
ding or crushing. Nonetheless, cats are still tied to the animal nutri-
al requirements for proteins, fats and carbohydrates. Prey animals
`ide cats' requirements for proteins and fats but carbohydrates are
lable only from plants. To meet their requirements for carbohydrates,
eat the partially digested plant material in the digestive tracts of their
nivorous prey.

 cats and lynxes have identical dental formulae of their 28 teeth. Puma
 30 teeth, having 3 upper premolars on each side. The smaller num-
 of cheek teeth found in felids compared to canids is consistent with
 s being more carnivorous. Felids' cheek teeth emphasize the carnas-
, which are the largest teeth in their mouths.

Order Cetartiodactyla
Even-toed hooved mammals and whales
Family Cervidae

Deer — white-tailed deer, moose, wapiti, caribou

Even-toed hooved mammals walk on just two toes of each foot. In evolution of these mammals, the big toes and thumbs were lost fir animals evolved to walk on the bottoms of four toes, much as dogs cats do today. Evolution then led to mammals with small second fifth toes that did not touch the ground. Ultimately, hooves evolved cover the tips of these two remaining, third and fourth toes on each f The fetlocks we see on the sides of deer feet are all that is left of t second and fifth toes. Almost all the terrestrial species in this Order evolved long, skinny legs adapted for running fast and evading preda All members of these terrestrial species are prey.

Interestingly, one branch within this Order, a branch that shares a c mon ancestor with the hippopotamus, evolved into the whales. Fo show how an ancient mammal species with early adaptations for run had a series of descendant species that evolved to forage in shallow w then in deep water and then evolved into species that constitute our p ent whales and dolphins, which live their whole lives swimming in w

A branch of the Cetartiodactyla evolved complex digestive systems c ble of digesting leaves and other plant parts that have complex cell w Mammals within this branch, including all members of the deer far are called ruminants because their digestive tracts include a chan called a rumen. The rumen is an outgrowth at the base of a rumin esophagus. It houses a complex mixture of bacteria that digest the walls of plants, thereby releasing the nutrients inside the cells for re nants to digest. All ruminants are herbivores.

Members of the deer family are distinguished by growing antlers. An are boney growths on the heads of males, and also of female caribou, grow each year but are then shed to grow anew the next year. Altho antlers usually regrow bigger during each of a deer's first few years, n tion has the greatest effect on antler size, then genetics, and finally One can not age a white-tailed deer or wapiti from the number of t on its antlers.

Antlers differ from horns, which members of the cow family (or a lope family) grow on their heads. First, antlers regrow and are shed year, while horns are permanent. Second, antlers grow from flat-top

jections on the skulls, called pedicels, and are covered with velvet-like
that provides blood and nutrition for the growing antlers. Horn cov-
are shed occasionally, exposing a bony core. When the horn covers
ow, they grow from the inside out, not from the outside in, as do ant-
. Third, except for caribou, only males grow antlers; both males and
ale cows and antelopes grow horns, though females' horns are smaller
n males'. In the North Woods, our members of the deer family begin
wing antlers in late winter to early spring, have antlers full grown by
-autumn, and shed their antlers in early- to mid-winter.

ite-tailed deer and moose have 32 teeth. Wapiti and caribou each have
ubby upper canine on each side of the mouth, giving them 34 teeth.
h cheek tooth of the cervids has a series of curved ridges, each ridge
ped much like a crescent-shaped moon, and the top and one edge of
h ridge are covered by enamel. The intervening valleys lack enamel,
osing the softer dentine tissue that is inside all teeth. Leaves, especially
sses, which incorporate silica in their tissues, are very abrasive. Over
e, abrasion from chewing plants wears down the enamel on the ridges
, because the valleys lack enamel, the valleys wear down a bit faster.
is uneven wear maintains the ridges and valleys on each tooth. Why
leaves not simply wear down the teeth? Ultimately, they do. But, for
st of each deer's life, the cheek teeth have open roots and continue to
w, just matching the speed at which the teeth are worn down.

four of our deer species in the North Woods breed in autumn, main-
pregnancies during winter, and give birth in spring. Young are able
fend for themselves by the autumn breeding season of their birth year
, during good years for food, some young females might even breed.
st young females continue to associate with their mothers throughout
ir lives, forming matriarchal social groups that can come to include
ings and cousins of many ages. Maturing males often aggregate in
all bachelor herds. The breeding season is called the "rut."

e names of two deer species of the North Woods can be confusing. The
ne "moose" is derived from the Anishinaabe (Ojibwa Indian) name for
animal—*mooz*. In the Scandinavian countries, the name of what we
a moose is *elg*. Consequently, moose in Eurasia are sometimes called
rasian elk. "Elk," however, is a common name in North America for
deer that in Eurasia is called "red deer." To make the names even
re confusing, North American "elk" and Eurasian red deer have in the
t been considered to be the same species. We think these confusions
a good reason to drop the name "elk" in North America and, instead,
call our elk wapiti, a name derived from the Cree language.

Order Chiroptera

Bats

Family Vespertilionidae

Evening Bats — little brown bat, red bat, hoary bat, big brown bat

Bats are the only mammals that fly. Bats' wings are made of skin stretch from their fingertips to their ankles, with added wing membranes t stretch from their wrists to their shoulders in front of their arms and fr their ankles to their tails behind their legs. The result is a highly flexi wing. As a rule, bats do not fly as fast as birds but are much more man verable. We have watched Common Nighthawks streaking through spotlights shining on a bell tower in early evening, catching insects the wing. As darkness settles and the bats come out, twisting and turni catching insect after insect after insect within the beam of the spotlig the nighthawks leave. At night, bats out-maneuver and out-compete th avian rivals. Were bats active during daytime, however, they would easy prey for such bird predators as Cooper's and Sharp-shinned Haw

Bats are more diverse, with over 1100 species, than any other Or of mammals except the rodents. They fall into two groups: Macrochiroptera, literally the "big bats," which eat fruit and live only Eurasia, Africa and Australia; and the Microchiroptera, or "little ba which are found around the globe. Many microchiropterans eat inse which they catch on the wing using echolocation. Others, however, small fish, which they catch using echolocation to detect ripples on surfaces of ponds, or eat frogs, whose mating calls they can hear. So eat fruit and some eat nectar and pollinate flowers.

An insectivorous bat echolocates as it forages, sending high-pitch sounds forward and catching the sounds bouncing back. Bats trans sounds using their mouths and their noses, which has led to the evoluti of bat species with noses of bizarre shapes, some broad and convolut others pointed. The ears of echolocating bats are relatively huge a some have strange shapes. All echolocating bats have a projection ins the front of each ear, called the "tragus," which helps bats hear and d ferentiate sounds. As a bat approaches a target insect, it sends calls fas and faster to track the insect. When a bat reaches three feet from insect, echoes return to the bat in 0.006 seconds; closer to the ins they return in 0.0007 seconds. Bats can discriminate objects as slim a human hair.

Insectivorous bats will eat half their weight in insects each night dur summer. Lactating females can eat their full weight or more each nig

crunch insects, bats have cheek teeth with multiple, pointed cusps.

y bats overwinter in caves and some roost in caves during summer.
y, however, roost in tight places, such as between the peeling bark of
e and the tree trunk, in tree cavities, and within the walls of houses.
of many species take readily to roosting in man-made bat houses.
roost hanging upside down from their hind feet. Some bats migrate
arm climates in winter but many stay north, some hibernating in
s but others in hollow trees and other protected sites. These bats
fat during late summer and autumn and then let their metabolic
and body temperatures drop once they enter their winter roosts,
g energy.

have a bad reputation for carrying rabies. Like all other mammals
birds, bats can contract rabies and some bats appear not to be seri-
y affected by the infection. Nonetheless, few bats actually carry rabies
many bats have teeth so small that they can not puncture human
to transmit the disease. Domestic dogs and cats, foxes, raccoons and
nks are far more likely to carry rabies and are far more dangerous for
ole. Nonetheless, the danger of rabies should not be belittled, since
disease is deadly. If you see a bat abroad in daylight, be careful.

seven bat species found in the North Woods are all in the family of
ning bats, the Vespertilionidae. All of these bats are rapacious insect
rs. All these bats also have reproductive adaptations that allow them
ave energy during winter. They mate during late summer or autumn,
r having experienced the food abundances of summer. This timing
ws females to choose mates at a time when males are healthy and best
to strut their stuff. Sperm, however, do not fertilize eggs right after
ing. Instead, sperm go dormant in each female's reproductive tract.
nales ovulate in spring after leaving hibernation, at which time the
m in their reproductive tracts become active and fertilize the eggs. A
rmal gestation and birth follow. Thus, females start the production of
ng as soon as they emerge from hibernation.

mbers of at least five of the bat species found in the North Woods
e been infected with the fungus that causes White-nose Syndrome
many populations have been decimated: big brown bat, little brown
long-eared bat, red bat, silver-haired bat. The fungus grows as a
y white patch on the nose, and often elsewhere on the body, of an
cted bat. In winter, infected bats come out of hibernation, forcing
m to burn the fat that they need for surviving till spring. The fungus
first observed on bats in northeastern US in the mid-2000s and
e has spread to the North Woods, including Minnesota's Soudan
derground Mine State Park where 10-15,000 bats hibernate.

Order Lagomorpha
Rabbits, Hares and Pikas
Family Leporidae

Rabbits & Hares — snowshoe hare, white-tailed jackrabbit, cotto

The Order Lagomorpha includes the rabbits, hares and pikas. All
species of pikas are in the Family Ochotonidae. Only two species
in North America and neither lives close to the North Woods. Thus
the lagomorphs in the North Woods are rabbits and hares, which co
tute the Family Leporidae. Rabbits and hares are similar in having l
ears and excellent hearing, to avoid predators, long hind feet to run
and to escape from predators, short tails, and teeth and a digestive t
adapted for processing vegetation. Rabbits and hares differ in that rab
are more compact with legs and ears long but not extreme, have yo
born naked with eyes and ears closed, and have species ranges that c
rarely extend into Canada. Hares are generally lanky with long ears
legs, their young are born furred with eyes and ears open, and the ra
of several extend far north.

Rabbits and hares have high reproductive rates and are capable
producing several litters in a year when nutritious food is abund
Consequently, many mammalian and avian predators prey on th
mammals. When rabbit and hare populations fall, however, the pre
tors find themselves with a food shortage. The predators search hard
the remaining rabbits or hares, depressing the lagomorph populati
further, followed by drops in the predator populations. Young rab
and hares are called leverets.

All rabbits and hares have 28 teeth and the same dental formula.
central, or first, upper incisors match the lower incisors in being v
large and able to chew plant material, including bark and small branc
The second upper incisors are small and nestled behind the large, cen
incisors. The cheek teeth have distinct enamel ridges with valleys betw
lacking enamel. The softer dentine that is exposed in the valleys we
down faster than the enamel, making teeth that can shred vegetati
Like the cheek teeth of deer and rodents, lagomorph cheek teeth h
open roots for most of a rabbit's or hare's life and continue growing
they wear down.

Because all lagomorphs are completely herbivorous, they have the sa
problem that deer and many rodents have: they must get their nutrit
from plants, whose cell walls are made of cellulose, which no mam
can digest. Like ruminants, a lagomorph has a chamber within its dig

tract that houses bacteria that can digest cellulose, releasing the
itious material inside of the plant cells. In lagomorphs, this chamber
lled the caecum. Unlike a ruminant, however, a lagomorph has its
um not at the front of the digestive tract but at the other end, at the
nning of the large intestine, also called the colon. The small intestine,
h lies between the stomach and the large intestine, absorbs nutrients
the colon absorbs mostly just water. This arrangement means that
bacteria that release nutrients for lagomorphs do so past the place
e the nutrients can be absorbed. A lagomorph's caecum, however,
ses its partially digested plant parts in globs that stay together travel-
through the colon. A lagomorph feels those globs moving to the end
e colon and re-ingests them directly from the anus, thereby sending
n for a second trip through the digestive tract. This action is often
d *coprophagy*, which means "eating feces," but this name is incorrect
use lagomorphs do not eat their feces; they eat caecal material and
digestive waste. Coprophagy is actually more efficient at releasing
ients than is rumination.

ne North Woods, we have three lagomorph species: eastern cottontail
bbit), the most widespread, snowshoe hare, the northernmost spe-
and white-tailed jackrabbit, which is Great Plains species and which,
ite its common name, is a hare.

rder Rodentia

dents

Order Rodentia has more species (over 2000), more families (about
and more individual animals spread more widely around the world
any other mammal group. Seven families have representative species
he North Woods. These seven families include one of the biggest
ents, the beaver, weighing up to 65 pounds. They include some of
smallest rodents, deer mice and pine voles, with some weighing less
half an ounce. And these families include some of the most striking
ents, our two chipmunk species.

lents are diverse but all have one common characteristic: a pair of
e incisors at the front of both upper and lower jaws and no other
sors, followed by a large space with no teeth, called the diastema. The
er incisors are more tightly curved than the lower incisors. These
ng incisors allow rodents to eat a huge range of plant foods. They
allow beavers to chew down trees.

st rodents are herbivores or omnivores, adding insects to a diet of
it parts. Just about every part of plants from leaves to bark to fruit

to seeds is eaten somewhere, at some time, by some rodent. In N
America, the grasshopper mice even prey on other small rodents
howl to warn other grasshopper mice away. Grasshopper mice do not
in the North Woods, so you do not have to worry about them (and
weigh less than an ounce).

Many rodents have common names that include "rat" or "mouse." Nei
rats nor mice form a taxonomic group and the words have no evolutio
implications. A mouse is simply a small rodent with a long tail; a r
a slightly larger small rodent with a long tail. Deer *mice* are more clo
related evolutionarily to cotton *rats* than they are to house *mice*.

Rodents disperse seeds of many plants and support diverse populat
of mammalian and avian predators. Without rodents, the world wo
not be the same.

Family Castoridae

Beavers — North American beaver

Although several beaver species lived in the past, only two species o
today, the North American species, *Castor canadensis*, and the Eura
species, *Castor fiber*. Members of the two species have very similar
histories and biology.

Beavers are responsible for much of the European exploration
settlement of North America. By the 1700s, Eurasian beavers had b
over-hunted across much of their range because their fur was so valua
French, Dutch and English explorers reported abundant beaver pop
tions in North America and established trapping and trading for be
pelts to be shipped to Europe. By the late 1800s, beavers were rar
North America as well. Protection in both North America and Eur
has allowed partial recovery of populations on both continents.

Beavers are often called ecosystem engineers because of their abili
to modify wetlands and surrounding terrestrial environments. Be
European settlement, North American beavers lived throughout
continent wherever year-round water existed or could be established
damming waterways. Beavers dropped trees and shrubs into water eve
where they lived and dammed every waterway that could be damm
Thus, *every* waterway (really, *every* waterway) in North America
affected by beavers, meaning that almost every single lake or stream
the continent exists now in a condition very different from its condit
before European colonization of North America. All streams flo
through series of dams, all lakes, rivers and streams had fallen trees al

edges, affecting water flow and the environment for aquatic organ-
. The same must have been true in Eurasia before the Eurasian beaver
lations were nearly extirpated.

mily Erethizontidae

World Porcupines — North American porcupine

e than a dozen species of porcupines live in the Americas, but only
porcupine lives in North America. The South and Central American
upines are smaller than the North American porcupine and most of
h have prehensile tails. All have quills that protect them from predators.

ls are modified guard hairs that are stiff, very sharp, and loosely
red in their follicles. The tip of a quill easily penetrates skin and a
ator with a face filled with quills is unable to continue an attack.
ls are barbed, in a manner, but not like fish hooks. Think of quills
eing covered with microscopic, overlapping roofing shingles whose
oms are not flat across but end in points. When a quill tip enters skin,
hundreds of little, back-facing shingles prevent the quill from being
cted easily. Skin movement tends to work a quill deeper and deeper.
cupines do not throw their quills.

ls are remarkably clean and seldom cause infection. Because they
najor irritants, they do cause inflammation, swelling and they hurt.
ators with many quills in their mouths and faces often die of starva-
because they are unable to kill and eat prey.

mily Cricetidae

World Cricetids — rats, mice, voles, muskrat, lemmings

New World rats, mice, voles and lemmings, the cricetids, are not
icted to the Americas but few cricetid species live in Eurasia, Africa
Australia. Just as the words "rat" and "mouse" describe approximate
y size and nothing else of importance, the words "mouse," "vole"
"lemming" describe approximate tail length. A vole is a mouse with
ort tail; a lemming is a vole with a shorter tail.

oss the Americas, cricetids are diverse. Muskrats are large, weighing
o four pounds, and live in marshes and other wetlands. Tree voles are
ll, weighing an ounce or less, and spend their entire lives in trees. Other
etids occupy nearly every habitat in the Americas that supports plants.

North Woods supports nine cricetid species, including white-footed
deer mice, muskrat, several species of voles and lemmings. Across

the region, you will see muskrat lodges in marshes and you may find
deer mice or white-footed mice would like to share the warmth of
house in winter. The voles and lemmings largely keep to themselves

Most of these rodents are prolific reproducers. Females begin bree
when the first green vegetation appears in spring. If food is abun
when the first litter is born, females will breed again within a day (c.
"post-partum breeding") and produce a second litter shortly after
young from the first litter can fend for themselves, at about four weel
age. With repeated post-partum breeding, females can produce sever
many litters during a summer and autumn in years with abundant fr

All the North Woods cricetids have the same dental formula of the
teeth. All have the typical, big incisors. White-footed and deer mice
molars with rounded cusps for chewing diverse foods from grasses
leaves to seeds and fruits to insects. The molars of the voles, inclu
muskrats, have looping enamel ridges across the top of each molar
excel at shredding and grinding vegetation. As for deer, rabbits and h
for most of each cricetid's life, the cheek teeth have open roots and
tinue to grow, just matching the speed at which the teeth are worn do

Having deer mice or white-footed mice in your house in winter is n
major problem. These mice are downright cute, with their big eyes,
ears, and sparkling whiskers. When we live-trap these mice with col
classes, we let the mice climb around on students' shoulders, arms
heads. The mice are friendly and are not destructive to houses, as ho
mice can be. Yes, they will eat food that you leave out on the kitc
counter, they do leave droppings, and they can build glorious nests fr
toilet paper or paper towels left where they can shred them. These inc
veniences, however, are not as important as the tiny gaps and heat le
in your house that their presence documents. A tight house will nor
these mice in when the weather turns cold and a tight house will save
a bundle on your winter heating bill.

If you do have deer mice or white-footed mice in your house or gar
you must take care when cleaning. These mice can carry a hanta v
that humans occasionally contract to become seriously ill. People do
contract the virus from the mice themselves but from dried feces a
urine that is lifted into dust that rises and is breathed when sweepi
If you have deer mice or white-footed mice in your garage or baseme
keep the areas clean and wear a mask when sweeping if you raise any d

nily Muridae

World Rats and Mice — brown rat, house mouse

Old World rats and mice include over 500 species. Members of these
ies have adaptations to live in the diverse habitats of Eurasia, Africa
Australia, from rain forests to desert to tundra. Some of these species
ved adaptations that allowed them to live with, and to obtain food
shelter from, humans. These species are often described as "com-
sal," meaning that they obtain resources from members of another
ies, in this case humans, without causing that other species any sig-
ant inconvenience. Most people, however, think of the relationship
veen rats and mice and humans more as parasitic.

"commensal" mice and rats in Eurasia evolved to co-exist with
le tens of thousands of years ago. They stole food from people
gained protection from predators by living and hiding near people.
en Eurasians began exploring the globe, ʒe rats and mice hitchhiked
them. Early on, Polynesian rats sailed with humans throughout
Pacific Ocean. Black rats, brown rats and house mice traveled across
ʒsia starting hundreds of years before Europeans took them to the
ericas, Australia and all the islands between. International commerce
huge container ships now disperses these rats and mice everywhere.

rnational commerce has distributed these rats and mice so thoroughly
nd the globe that extensive hybridization now obscures phylogenetic
kgrounds of species to the point that here in North America, we can
tify a hybrid swarm of Old World rats, with genes from black rats
tus rattus), brown rats (*R. norvegicus*) and at least two other Asian spe-
We also have a hybrid swarm of Old World house mice, including
es of *Mus musculus* and *M. domesticus*.

molars have rounded cusps that are good for crushing and grinding
rse foods.

nily Sciuridae

irrels — chipmunks, woodchuck, tree squirrels, flying squirrels

Sciuridae, the squirrel family, is large and we have ten species in the
th Woods. Squirrels are known for their climbing abilities and even
ground squirrels are capable climbers. Squirrels can rotate their ankles
hat their hind feet face upward when they descend trees headfirst.

irrel species fall into three groups, all of which have representatives
ʒe North Woods: ground squirrels, tree squirrels and flying squirrels.
ground squirrels include the least chipmunk, eastern chipmunk,

woodchuck and Franklin's and thirteen-lined ground squirrels. ˈ squirrels include the red, gray and fox squirrels. Flying squirrels inc the northern and southern flying squirrels.

All squirrels are basically herbivorous but gain additional nutrit sometimes critical nutrition, from fungi, large insects and insect la and even small vertebrates. Most of our squirrels have 22 teeth, thou few have only 1 upper premolar on each side for a total of 20 teeth. large incisors allow these rodents to eat a diversity of nuts and seed open thick shells of seeds, such as hickories and walnuts, and to c conifer cones. The cheek teeth have rounded cusps for crushing grinding foods, many of which are reasonably soft once their shells removed.

Family Zapodidae

Jumping Mice — meadow jumping mouse, woodland jumping mo

The jumping mice, or zapodids, are well adapted for jumping. All long hind feet, for the jumps, and long tails, to help steer. We have species in North America, and two in the North Woods. Their cl relatives outside North America are the jerboas and birch mice of Eu and northern Africa, most of whom live in deserts. Some data sug that our North American jumping mice should be included with Eurasian relatives in the Family Dipodidae.

Jumping mice mostly forage walking on all four feet but their big feet can catapult three to four yards and away from predators. Get good at using those hind feet requires practice, however. We once fo ourselves in the midst of a litter of at least five young meadow jum mice that were practicing their jumps. Some jumps went up only, s went long, and many left one youngster piling into a litter mate, sen both a-tumble. We stood stock still, enjoying the show while strugg not to laugh.

Meadow jumping mice have 18 teeth, but woodland jumping lack the little, upper premolars, giving them 16 teeth. The molars rounded cusps for crushing and grinding vegetation and insects. upper incisor has a distinct longitudinal groove in front. The functic the groove is not known but such a groove should increase strength tooth to resist twisting.

rder Soricimorpha

rews and moles

soricimorphs, or shrew-shaped mammals, forage for the insects and
r invertebrates that live just above and just below the surface of the
nd. Shrews are such small mammals that most of them make deer
look large. They have very pointed muzzles, tiny feet, and velvety
with guard hairs that do not have a nap, letting shrews back up in
places. They forage for insects or other invertebrates on the surface
e ground within the litter on the forest floor and within grasslands.
es are larger, more the size of a chipmunk. Moles, too, have pointed
zles and guard hairs with no nap, but have very large feet for digging.
y forage in tunnels they dig just under the ground surface. Shrews
moles have five toes on each foot.

hrews and moles are difficult to observe because they live under the
ce litter and under ground. All are solitary and active year round.

se mammals are generally called "insectivores" because that word is
conventional and easier to say than "invertebrativores," which is
e accurate.

nily Soricidae

ews — arctic shrew, common shrew, pygmy shrew, short-tailed
w and other shrews

ws are very small mammals with very pointed muzzles, small eyes
ear pinnae, small feet, and velvety fur with guard hairs that do
have a nap, letting shrews back up in tight places. They forage for
rtebrates on the surface of the ground and within the litter on for-
loor and within grasslands. They have teeth well adapted to kill and
rocess invertebrates. All shrews in the North Woods have the same
al formula and 32 teeth. All teeth are dark burgundy-colored at their
The 1st upper incisors are large and protruding, and are used to stab
. The rest of the teeth are pointed, with the molars having several,
ted cusps.

have six shrew species in the North Woods and they fall into two groups.
long-tailed shrews are very small, skinny, and have tails that are usu-
⅓ to ½ of their total lengths. These shrews are generally a variation
rown to gray in color. Our one short-tailed shrew species, the north-
short-tailed shrew, or simply short-tailed shrew, is the size of a small
se, is gray, and has a tail that is usually less than ¼ of its total length.

Shrews must eat diverse invertebrates to balance their diets. They us~~ eat just half of large items, like an earthworm or grasshopper, and begin foraging for other foods needed to balance their diets. To fuel t high metabolic rates, shrews forage day and night. Their foraging b last less than an hour, separated by shorter resting periods. Little el known about the life histories and behavior of most shrews.

Predators sometimes kill shrews and then leave them on gravel roads

Family Talpidae

Moles — eastern mole, star-nosed mole, hairy-tailed mole

Moles are small mammals with very pointed muzzles, small eyes, n~ pinnae, huge forefeet, short tails and velvety fur with guard hairs tha not have a nap, letting moles back up in tight places. They forage invertebrates under the surface of the ground and have teeth well ada to kill and to process invertebrates. Their teeth are pointed, with molars having several pointed cusps. Star-nosed moles have 44 teeth, eastern moles have 36 teeth.

We have two mole species in the North Woods, the eastern mole anc star-nosed mole. Both are easy to identify. No other mammals have relatively huge feet, which the moles use for digging their tunnels under the ground surface. Their tunnels are often so close to the su~ that they elevate the surface, leaving humped roofs over the tun Some suburbanites complain that moles eat the roots of their grass, w is not true because moles are completely insectivorous. Tunnels nea~ ground surface can cause grass roots to dry, however, which someti does kill grass. By and large, however, moles aerate the soil and eat in tebrates that sometimes eat grass and grass roots. Like shrews, mole~ diverse invertebrates to balance their diets.

Moles dig using a motion called "rotation thrust." Moles have un shoulder blades and upper arm bones allowing them to rotate the u foreleg around its long axis while the lower foreleg, held at a right a~ shoves dirt backwards. To understand how this movement works, an arm straight out, parallel to the ground. Then rotate the arm an~ your forearm hang straight down, your hand at the bottom, with upper arm still parallel to the ground. Now, without changing elbow position, rotate your arm at your shoulder so that your hand p~ es back. Imagine that you are pushing dirt backwards with your h That is what moles do. Moles' shoulder blades and upper arm bones humerus) are shaped very differently from ours, making rotation th digging the most powerful digging done by any mammal.

Dental Formulae for North Woods Mammals

...ssum	$I\frac{5}{4}\ C\frac{1}{1}\ P\frac{3}{3}\ M\frac{4}{4}$ =50		Tricolored Bat	$I\frac{2}{3}\ C\frac{1}{1}\ P\frac{2}{2}\ M\frac{3}{3}$ =34
...lf, Fox, ...yote	$I\frac{3}{3}\ C\frac{1}{1}\ P\frac{4}{4}\ M\frac{2}{3}$ =42		Big Brown Bat	$I\frac{2}{3}\ C\frac{1}{1}\ P\frac{1}{2}\ M\frac{3}{3}$ =32
...unks	$I\frac{3}{3}\ C\frac{1}{1}\ P\frac{3}{3}\ M\frac{1}{2}$ =34		Hoary Bat, Red Bat	$I\frac{1}{3}\ C\frac{1}{1}\ P\frac{2}{2}\ M\frac{3}{3}$ =32
...rten, ...her, ...lverine	$I\frac{3}{3}\ C\frac{1}{1}\ P\frac{4}{4}\ M\frac{1}{2}$ =38		Rabbits, Hares	$I\frac{2}{1}\ C\frac{0}{0}\ P\frac{3}{2}\ M\frac{3}{3}$ =28
...asels, ...dger	$I\frac{3}{3}\ C\frac{1}{1}\ P\frac{3}{3}\ M\frac{1}{2}$ =34		Beaver	$I\frac{1}{1}\ C\frac{0}{0}\ P\frac{1}{1}\ M\frac{3}{3}$ =20
...er	$I\frac{3}{3}\ C\frac{1}{1}\ P\frac{4}{3}\ M\frac{1}{2}$ =36		Porcupine	$I\frac{1}{1}\ C\frac{0}{0}\ P\frac{1}{1}\ M\frac{3}{3}$ =20
...coon	$I\frac{3}{3}\ C\frac{1}{1}\ P\frac{4}{4}\ M\frac{2}{2}$ =40		Mice, Rats, Voles, Lemmings	$I\frac{1}{1}\ C\frac{0}{0}\ P\frac{0}{0}\ M\frac{3}{3}$ =16
...ck Bear	$I\frac{3}{3}\ C\frac{1}{1}\ P\frac{4}{4}\ M\frac{2}{3}$ =42		Fox & Red Squirrel, Chipmunks	$I\frac{1}{1}\ C\frac{0}{0}\ P\frac{1}{1}\ M\frac{3}{3}$ =20
...cat, ...x	$I\frac{3}{3}\ C\frac{1}{1}\ P\frac{2}{2}\ M\frac{1}{1}$ =28		Most Squirrels	$I\frac{1}{1}\ C\frac{0}{0}\ P\frac{2}{1}\ M\frac{3}{3}$ =22
...a	$I\frac{3}{3}\ C\frac{1}{1}\ P\frac{3}{2}\ M\frac{1}{1}$ =30		Meadow Jumping Mouse	$I\frac{1}{1}\ C\frac{0}{0}\ P\frac{1}{0}\ M\frac{3}{3}$ =18
...r, Moose	$I\frac{0}{3}\ C\frac{0}{1}\ P\frac{3}{3}\ M\frac{3}{3}$ =32		Woodland Jumping Mouse	$I\frac{1}{1}\ C\frac{0}{0}\ P\frac{0}{0}\ M\frac{3}{3}$ =16
...iti, ...bou	$I\frac{0}{3}\ C\frac{1}{1}\ P\frac{3}{3}\ M\frac{3}{3}$ =34		Shrews	$I\frac{3}{1}\ C\frac{1}{1}\ P\frac{3}{1}\ M\frac{3}{3}$ =32
...e Brown, ...t-eared	$I\frac{2}{3}\ C\frac{1}{1}\ P\frac{3}{3}\ M\frac{3}{3}$ =38		Eastern Mole	$I\frac{3}{2}\ C\frac{1}{0}\ P\frac{3}{3}\ M\frac{3}{3}$ =36
...r-haired	$I\frac{2}{3}\ C\frac{1}{1}\ P\frac{2}{3}\ M\frac{3}{3}$ =36		Star-nosed Mole	$I\frac{3}{3}\ C\frac{1}{1}\ P\frac{4}{4}\ M\frac{3}{3}$ =44

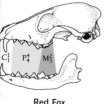

$I\frac{1}{1}\ C\frac{1}{1}\ P\frac{4}{4}\ M\frac{2}{3}$

Red Fox

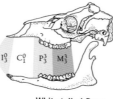

$I\frac{0}{3}\ C\frac{0}{1}\ P\frac{3}{3}\ M\frac{3}{3}$

White-tailed Deer

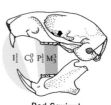

$I\frac{1}{1}\ C\frac{0}{0}\ P\frac{1}{1}\ M\frac{3}{3}$

Red Squirrel

...ing dental formulae can help you identify mammals by their skulls. In any formula ...isor, C=canine, P=premolar, M=molar with teeth numbers for one half of the jaw. ...xample, $I\frac{2}{3}$ means that this mammal has two incisors on each side of the upper jaw ...hree incisors on each side of the lower jaw. The total number of teeth is double the ...ers in the formula because it includes all teeth on both sides of the mouth.

How to use this Field Guide

Order

The only marsupial living in the North Woods, the Virginia oposs is the first mammal species presented; thereafter, mammals are grou taxonomically by Order, handled alphabetically. Within each Or mammals are listed by Family, which are grouped alphabetically ex when physical similarities suggested a different grouping (for exam all Families of mice are grouped together). Within Families, mamm are grouped alphabetically by scientific name unless, again, similar suggest a different grouping.

Mammal Names

Every species of mammal has a single scientific name, like *Canis lupu* the wolf and *Castor canadensis* for the beaver. In contrast, no mamm have official common names. Consequently, some people call memb of the species *Puma concolor* cougar, others call them puma and o people call them mountain lion. All names are equally correct. In guide, we include multiple common names for species that have the

Photos

We have picked photos that show basic field marks, typical poses normal behaviors for each species. The vast majority of photos show living, wild individuals; we used photos of captive mammals only w no wild images were available.

Habitat

The most common habitats for each species are listed below the photo. Those habitats provide your best chances for finding membe a given species—but not exclusively. Some species have narrow hal requirements while others are quite flexible in their uses of habitats.

Nature Notes

Nature Notes are fascinating bits of natural history that round out understanding of a species. Population trends, ecology, naming his and other information are included.

Size

We give average sizes for weight (female and male where sexual din phism is great), body length, total length, tail length. Measurement in US ounces, pounds, inches, feet.

Range

The North American range for a species is described briefly in this sec and a map shows range in the North Woods.

wing Tips

s and ideas on how get the best views for a particular species.

ssary

y to understand meanings for some tricky terms.

es of Interest

ese titles may be of interest to you as you develop a passion for mam-
s; books about tracking, ecology, natural history and more.

Young Readers

the budding naturalist or mammalogist, this is a brief selection of the
nors' favorite books for young readers. Readers of all ages will reap
ards from sharing books like these with friends and family members.
se good books introduce readers to all kinds of mammals, as well as
er animals, through stories, poems and striking illustrations.

ture Notes
natural history
pits about this
cies.

The main photo is a diagnos-
tic image of this species.
Sometimes a close up showing
more detail can be found at
the bottom of the page.

Additional photos may show
juveniles, behavior, other
color phases, seasonal
dimorphism, tracks, prey,
etc.

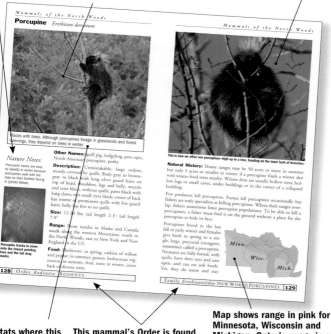

itats where this
nmal typically
urs.

This mammal's Order is found
on the left footer and Family
shown on the right footer.

Map shows range in pink for
Minnesota, Wisconsin and
Michigan. Ontario range is only
shown for species with a very
limited range in the American
North Woods.

Virginia Opossum *Didelphis virginiana*

Found mostly in deciduous forest near water but also wooded urban are̶

Nature Notes:

Our own all-American marsupial.

Possums sometimes become temporarily catatonic, called "playing possum," when threatened. They also freeze in bright lights, leading to highway mortalities.

Baby opossums are called "joeys."

Other Names: o'possum, Virginia o'poss̶ North American possum, possum

Description: Size of a very large domestic̶ but low to the ground; body gray with bl̶ gray and white guard hairs; white unde̶ shows through guard hairs; prehensile tail l̶ scaly with sparse guard hairs. Gait slow, s̶ fling, with a twist with each step.

Size: Male weight 6 lbs; female weight 4̶ total length 20-35″; tail length 8-13″

Range: Southeast US north to New Engl̶ and south through Mexico; also along̶ Pacific coast of the US.

Food: Omnivore: fruits, nuts, grains, wo̶ other large invertebrates, small mammals, b̶ and eggs, carrion.

Natural History: The North Woods co̶ tutes the northern limit to possum distribut̶ possums here often freeze their ears and tip̶ their tails in winter. The frozen tissue dies̶

Possums are slowly moving north into the North Woods, but hairless ears and tails are not well suited to extreme cold.

eventually sloughs, leaving many with short ears with jagged, black edges and short, blunt tails.

Rest and escape sites include holes in the ground, under roots, in rock crevices and under porches. Breeding in spring. Gestation lasts about 12 days, after which time young move to the pouch where each attaches to one of 13 teats. Young stay attached to teats for 8 to 9 weeks and are weaned at 3-3½ months.

Possum urine contains sulphur bearing compounds that have an odor reminiscent of skunk smell and of fox urine. Possum urine is distinctly sweet smelling, however, and, with some practice, is easy to differentiate from the scents of skunks and foxes.

Behavior: Possums use their prehensile tails and opposable big toes when climbing among small tree branches to harvest fruit. They can hang from their tails.

Viewing Tips: Possums most often forage at night. You might find them on your back porch eating dog or cat food or raiding a platform bird feeder. During the day, you can smell possum urine near frequently used rest sites.

Minn.

Wisc.

Mich.

Coyote   *Canis latrans*

Coyotes live in all habitats from forest to agricultural areas to cities. Wherever they live, they excel at hiding from people.

Nature Notes:

Resourceful, flexible predator.

Also known as "brush wolf," but it is not a gray or timber wolf.

Wolves kill coyotes when they can. Where wolves are common, coyotes spend most of their time along wolf pack boundaries, thereby avoiding wolves.

Other Names: brush wolf

Description: Resembles a medium-large d usually with grizzled, reddish brown c sometimes gray to black; tail long and full; large and pointed; distinct muzzle; nose small compared to wolf; legs long and sli compared to wolf. Males average larger th females.

Size: Male weight 25-30 lbs; female wei 20-25 lbs; total length 3-5'; tail length 1½'

Range: Found throughout Central and No America except Labrador, northern Que and the High Arctic in Canada. Before No America was colonized by Europeans, coyo lived only in southwest North America a northern Mexico. Coyotes have since coloni the rest of North and Central America, es cially moving into areas where wolves had b extirpated.

...tes listen for the rusting of small mammals in grass or under snow, then pounce on their ...specting prey.

...te pair scent marking.

...od: Carnivore to Omnivore: rabbits and hares, ground squirrels, tree ...rrels, occasionally deer; in summer fruit, garden vegetables and, in ...es, food from dumpsters. Will scavenge dead prey and garbage. In ...cultural areas, some coyotes learn to kill livestock, especially sheep ... goats. Coyotes are often blamed for killing livestock that have actu-...been killed by domestic ...s.

...tural History: Coyotes ...ally maintain pair bonds ...t last years. They exhibit ...ible social organization ...n mostly solitary to main-...ing packs. These packs are ...ended families with a pair ...parents and offspring from

Though this encounter looks ferocious, it is not a fight but rather dominance behavior between pack mates.

recent years. The social organization of coyotes depends mostly on abundance, diversity and distribution of major foods in any given a Where coyotes prey mostly on small prey, such as voles, mice and rabb they usually forage singly. Where the predominant prey are large, coyo are more likely to live in packs. Home ranges vary in size, usually with abundance of food, and can be as large as tens of square miles. Meml of a pack all share the same home range.

Coyotes breed in mid-winter. When they live in packs, the parent coyo are the only ones who breed. After about 9 weeks of gestation, pups born in a den that is often a small cave or hole dug in a bank. Dur autumn, pups within packs begin to travel with the rest of the pack hunting forays. Where coyotes do not live in packs, pups begin to perse in autumn to find spaces without resident coyotes of their own where they can settle. Coyotes usually reach sexual maturity at 10 mon of age.

Where coyote populations are low, some coyotes breed with dome dogs, producing hybrids called "coydogs." Although coydogs someti behave much like domestic dogs, their behavior can be unpredictable a they do not make good pets. Coydogs are not able to breed with coyo because coydogs of both sexes are seasonally sexually active at a differ time of year than are coyotes.

Behavior: Coyotes hunting singly concentrate foraging where prey abundant. They use a classic "mouse pounce" to catch mice and voles dense grass and under snow: a coyote leaps up, coming down with

paws on its prey. Where
[it] preys on deer, they
[must] attack cooperatively, as
[do] wolves, but some adults
[become] skilled at killing
[deer], and even wapiti, singly.
[No] matter what their diet,
[coyo]tes are adept at finding
[food] and learning new foods
[and] where to find them.

[Like] wolves, coyotes com-
[mun]icate with other pack
[mem]bers using postures,
[facia]l expressions and vocal-
[izati]ons. Parents and other
[adul]t pack members dem-
[ons]trate dominance over
[you]nger coyotes. Coyote
[pac]ks communicate with

Coyotes often live and hunt in packs in the North Woods where prey can be large.

[oth]er packs using scent marks and by howling. When lone coyotes meet,
[they] communicate as do coyotes within packs.

[Vie]**wing Tips:** Keep your eyes open along rural roads, where coyotes
hunt for mice and voles in tall grass.

[Coyo]tes hunt in the daytime where they are not persecuted by humans.

Eastern Gray Wolf (Timber Wolf) *Canis lu[*

All habitats prior to European settlement. Today, forested areas and areas with agriculture mixed with forest.

Nature Notes:

Dogs have been domesticated from wolves. Though dogs differ from wolves in many ways, they communicate among themselves and with humans using most of the postures, facial expressions, vocalizations and scents of dominance and submission that wolves use.

Despite their common evolutionary background, wolves often kill dogs, as they kill coyotes. When you hike and camp in wolf country, keep your dog close so that it does not fall prey to wolves.

Other Names: gray wolf, timber wolf, wo[

Description: Resembles very large dog wi[grizzled brown to gray coat but can be whit[black; tail long and full; muzzle not as nar[and pointed as on coyote; ears compact a[pointed and not as prominent as on coy[eyes yellow; legs long with big feet, legs stu[compared to coyote. Males average larger t[females.

Size: Male weight 55-70 lbs; female weight 65 lbs; total length 5'; tail length 1-2'

Range: Formerly throughout most of Eura[and North America. In the United States, n[restricted to the Upper Great Lakes states, Rocky Mountains from the Yellowstone e[system north, and a small population in southwest.

Food: Carnivore: large hooved mammals; North Woods predominantly white-tailed d[

...s live in extended family units called packs. Nonpack wolves travel along boundaries to ...erritories.

...also moose, wapiti and caribou; in summer, beavers, snowshoe hares, ...occasional livestock.

...ural History: Wolves live in packs that are extended family units. ...1 pack has two parent wolves, sometimes called the alpha male and ...a female. Most other pack members are offspring wolves born into ...pack over the previous few years. Each pack maintains a territory ...is not shared with other wolves. Territories can be 50 square miles ...1uch larger.

...parent wolves are almost always the only wolves that breed in a ...:. They breed in late February and young are born about 9 weeks ...: in a den that is often ...1all cave or a hole dug ...bank. During the pups' ...two months, when their ...her is nursing them, other ...: members bring food to ...mother and pups. As pups ...n to eat solid food, pack ...1bers bring ingested food,

Wolf pups can look a bit scraggly before they grow into their adult fur coat.

which is regurgitated for the p When pups become mobile, the leaves the den and stays for var periods of time at a series of on several rendezvous sites, which often near water. During autu pups begin to travel with the re the pack on hunting forays. Wo usually reach sexual maturity a months of age.

Behavior: During much of the wolves in a pack hunt cooperati When a deer or other hooved man is killed, the parents eat first and o pack members share later. As the is eaten, legs, head and other b parts are removed from the carcass carried to private eating places. This system of hunting and eating g antees that the parents are the best fed members of a pack and, thus able to raise young each year. Young wolves may leave their packs as reach 2 or 3 years of age or older. Each will seek a place to establish a p of its own or to join a pack that has had one of its parent members o

Wolves communicate with other pack members using postures, f expressions and vocalizations. Parent wolves and other adult pack m bers demonstrate dominance over younger wolves, which affects ea hierarchies. Subtle, quiet vocalizations are not well understood. Wo tell other packs to stay out of their territory using scent marks and howling. Wolves scent mark using urine, feces, and secretions from glands and other glands, such as glands on their feet. Wolves selo howl when pups are young. Once a pack moves to a rendezvous site, wolves howl most commonly when they have something to defend, s as a kill. A pack will often howl in response to hearing another pack he

Wolves and ravens have a special relationship; ravens help wolves find unopened carcass and ravens benefit by getting to eat some wolf-killed prey.

wing Tips: Wolves often howl in response to sirens, train whistles even to humans who howl. When you are within wolf range, try ·ling on a still evening and wait quietly for wolves to respond. If a ̇ is nearby, they usually respond within five minutes, and sometimes ·ond immediately. Alternately, a single wolf might respond. If you ̇ at 10 to 15 minute intervals, you might get the wolf to howl often, ·ving you by sound the route he or she follows through the woods.

·lack color phase is more common in the Greater Yellowstone Ecosystem than in the Woods.

·f wolves on the ice of Lake Superior. This is how wolves reached Michigan's Isle Royale, ·ing nearly 20 miles over pack ice to reach the island and its healthy moose population.

·s will sometimes take part of their prey (deer leg, in this case) and carry it to a seclud- ·ot to eat in peace.

Red Fox *Vulpes fulva*

Red foxes inhabit most non-desert habitats.

Nature Notes:

Sharply-dressed predator.

Red foxes are curious and good at finding food. A red fox can harvest a significant portion of a rural garden.

Just as wolves often kill coyotes, coyotes often kill red foxes. Red foxes avoid coyote territories. Wolves tolerate red foxes, however, and the two species often live in the same areas.

Other Names: Formerly known as *V vulpes*

Description: Size of a medium-sized dog smaller than coyote; muzzle pointed, ears la pointed; legs and feet black, tail tip white. color phases: 1) Red phase; most common 100% of most populations; body and b tail red to orange-red, chin and chest w 2) Silver or black phase; up to 10% of fox some high latitude populations; black g hairs with white tips. 3) Cross phase; ur 25% of foxes in some high latitude populati reddish-brown with black shoulders. 4) Bas phase; rare; body gray-blue.

Size: Weight 8-14 lbs; total length 3-3½'; length 1-1½'

Range: Circumpolar in distribution; fc across much of Canada and the US, except sections of the West.

...ox with a still-living muskrat. This was in spring and the fox was likely taking this large ...back to the den to share with its pups. Foxes are carnivores with wide-ranging tastes.

...d: Carnivore: voles and mice, rabbits and hares, squirrels, birds, bird ..., turtle eggs; in summer fruit and garden vegetables.

...ural History: A pair of red foxes shares a territory that is often in the ...e of 10 to 15 square miles in size. Territories of different pairs do not ...lap and are maintained mostly through scent marking. Urine of red ...s contains sulphur-bearing compounds that have a smell reminiscent ...ut distinct from, skunk smell. Pungent scent marks can be smelled ...g trails and rural roads. These marks let you know that a fox uses the .... Unless you become an expert on scent, you will need to see the fox ...left its mark to know whether it is a red or a gray.

...e North Woods, red foxes ...d in mid-winter and give ...1 to 4-7 pups some 9 weeks ... in a den that may be ...ld woodchuck hole, some ...r hole in the ground or on ...nk, or a small cave. Both ...bers of the pair help to ... their pups, which may

Minn.

Wisc.

Mich.

Their incredible hearing allows red foxes to detect the movements of mice and voles under deep snow. A forceful pounce allows a fox to generate enough force to reach its subnivean meal.

remain with the parents for many months to nearly a year. Young female sometimes delay dispersal to help their parents raise the next litter, often in areas where some important foods are both localized and abundant enough to support more than just a pair of foxes.

Behavior: Red foxes usually hunt singly, concentrating their foraging where prey are abundant. They use a classic "mouse pounce" to catch mice and voles in dense grass and under snow: a red fox leaps up, comes down with its fore paws on its prey.

Like wolves and coyotes, red foxes communicate using postures, facial expressions and vocalizations. Red foxes mark with urine, feces and and other gland secretions.

After shedding their winter coats, summer red foxes can appear almost scrawny.

ewing Tips: During late spring, look for red fox dens in high banks
ve rural roads or perhaps in a gravel pit. In winter, follow fox tracks in
snow through a pasture or a year-old clear cut and count the number
imes that the fox mouse-pounces.

ies causes infrequent epizootics in red fox populations. Be aware of
h epizootics and avoid red foxes that exhibit odd behavior, such as
ng friendly towards humans.

ox on the left is a color phase known as "cross" fox; note the darker coloration and
k shoulder fur. All color phases of red fox show a white-tipped tail.

I cross" fox (left) is a color phase that shows some gold-red around the ears but little on the
. "Silver" fox is a color phase of the red fox that has black hairs tipped with silvery gray.

oxes can have "mixed" litters with some normally-colored young and some "cross" or
r" phase. Pups stay near the den until old enough to hunt on their own.

Gray Fox   *Urocyon cinereoargenteus*

Forests, including open forests, woodlots; farmland and suburban area with forest patches, especially with fruit trees.

Nature Notes:

Gray foxes can shinny up straight trees by holding around the sides of the trees with their forepaws and pushing up with their hind paws. They can jump from branch to branch in trees to reach fruit and go down head first.

Gray foxes have black tipped tails (red foxes' tails tipped in white), short muzzles and long necks.

Description: Smaller than red fox; back, and bushy tail grizzled gray, tip of tail bl orange to cinnamon patches on tail bott legs, sides and neck; muzzle short and poin ears large and pointed; the orange highlight gray foxes are not to be confused with the or red-orange backs of red foxes.

Size: Weight 8-14 lbs; total length 3'; length 1-1½'

Range: Found across the US except nort Great Plains and northern Rocky Mounta throughout Central America.

Food: Carnivore to omnivore: year rou rabbits, voles, mice; in summer, grasshopp crickets, fruit, garden vegetables.

Natural History: Home ranges are usu well under a square mile and are made kno to other gray foxes by scent marks. Urin gray foxes contains sulphur-bearing compou

...oxes sometimes frequent backyard bird feeders where they eat both sunflower seeds ...e voles and mice eating the sunflower seeds below the feeders.

have a smell reminiscent of, but distinct from, skunk smell. Pungent ...t marks can be smelled along trails and rural roads. Unless you ...me an expert on scent, you will need to see the fox that left its mark ...now whether it is a red or gray.

...y foxes breed in late winter and gestation is about 8½ weeks. A litter, ...lly 4 pups, is born in a den that is often a hole in a bank. Both par-...help raise the pups, which become independent at about 7 months ...e. Youngsters reach sexual maturity at about 10 months of age. Gray ...s usually breed every year.

...avior: Gray foxes are the least social of the North Woods canids and ...e independently except during breeding season.

...wing Tips: Gray foxes ...rally avoid humans but ...be seen at any time of the ...We have seen gray foxes ...idday, standing stock ...and staring back at us. ...y often come to winter ...feeders to feast on fallen ...ower seeds and the voles ...cted to the sunflower seeds.

Eastern Spotted Skunk   *Spilogale putorius*

Spotted skunks seldom forage in the open but prefer forested areas or grassland with overhead cover; farmland is also utilized.

Nature Notes:

Cute "master chemist" that is rarely seen.

Not recorded in Minnesota until 1914, and then its population boomed. Has declined drastically since the late 1940s, probably due to changing farming practices and loss of habitat in the rural landscape. Only two confirmed sightings in Minnesota in the last 20 years.

Spotted skunks seldom contract rabies, even though their striped cousins experience epizootics.

Its cousin, the western spotted skunk (*Spilogale gracilis*) ranges across the western US and northern Mexico.

Other Names: civet cat, little skunk, pole four-striped skunk, spotted skunk

Description: Smaller than striped sku body black with six prominent white str that break into spots on back; face with w patch on forehead; tail white mixed with bl

Size: Weight ¾ -1¼ lbs; total length 1½-2' length 8-10"

Range: Southeast US from Florida up so ern Appalachian Mountains, across Sout northern Mexico, north through the eas prairies and adjacent forests to northeas Minnesota.

Food: Omnivore: small mammals, birds eggs, carrion, fruit, seeds, insects and o invertebrates.

Natural History: Despite their chem defenses, they are occasional prey for G Horned Owls, coyotes, bobcats and foxes.

tted skunks breed annually in March and April but in years with ndant food, some females breed again in mid- to late summer, ducing another litter. Gestation is 7-9 weeks, varied due to delayed lantation. They den in dry holes in the ground, including those pre-1sly used by other mammals, and in crevices in trees.

havior: Eastern spotted skunks are good mousers and when mice and es are plentiful will have carnivorous diets. They are more carnivorous 1 striped skunks. Anecdotes suggest that spotted skunks can be quite ful.

e their big cousins, they warn by stamping their feet and chattering r teeth. Eastern spotted skunks will also stand on their fore paws as a ning. Once you find yourself facing the back end of a skunk with a ed tail, however, you are close to being beyond warning.

wing Tips: Spotted skunks are curious and willing to watch humans n a short distance. We have played hide and seek around a hollow tree re than once with a spotted skunk. If you stand still, a spotted skunk nlikely to blast you.

Striped Skunk *Mephitis mephitis*

Striped skunks are habitat generalists and live in prairies, grasslands, farmlands and forests. You can find them anywhere.

Nature Notes:

A direct spray in the face can cause temporary blindness, so be careful.

Mortality of young skunks can be high. Road kill mortality of adults is also high because skunks do not respond quickly to potential threats.

Rabies causes infrequent epizootics in striped skunk populations. Be aware of such epizootics and avoid skunks that exhibit odd behavior, such as being friendly towards humans.

Young skunk out and about.

Other Names: polecat

Description: Unmistakable; body black w prominent white stripes from head to tail, of stripes variable; face black with white sti from nose to white patch on head.

Size: 5-10 lbs; total length 2-2¾'; tail 8-12"

Range: Throughout most of North Ame from boreal forests of Canada to north Mexico, except for parts of the desert Southw

Food: Omnivore: small mammals, birds, e carrion, insects and other invertebrates (up to percent of diet), fruit, seeds, garden vegetabl

Natural History: Skunk spray is made paired anal glands, located on either side c skunk's anus, and contains a complex mixt of sulphur compounds. Descriptions of smell of these compounds range from smell like sewage or rotting food to smelling like c centrated garlic, none of which seem accurate

gh primarily nocturnal, occasionally striped skunks can be seen during daylight hours.

We actually like a dilute whiff on the wind. Nonetheless, all descrip-
s of the smell pale compared to the real thing in action.

pite their chemical defenses, skunks are occasional prey for Great
ned Owls and other raptors, hungry coyotes and, of course, domestic
s.

nks breed in mid- to late winter and give birth 2 to 2½ months later;
variation in gestation is caused by delayed implantation. Kits, often 5
, are born under root masses, in holes in the ground, in small caves,
nder buildings. Though nearly naked at birth, skunk kits already
w black and white color patterns on their skin. By 8 days old they are
ducing musk but they cannot aim until their eyes open at 3½ weeks.

nks exhibit winter lethargy in cold weather but not classic hiberna-
. Seldom seen in winter in the North Woods. They often share dens
elp keep warm.

navior: Warn predators, and people, by stamping their feet and chat-
ng their teeth before spraying.

wing Tips: Skunk spray
be difficult to remove
ause of its oiliness. Some
ple claim that dilute
ch cuts the odor. We can
e from experience that
ato juice does not. The
r does fade in time. Wear
s a badge of honor.

Wolverine   *Gulo gulo*

Wolverines are habitat generalists within boreal forests and tundra. They live where snow stays well into spring.

Nature Notes:

Wolverines are famous for raiding trappers' trap lines. Stories of their strength verge on myth and wolverines are often imagined to have qualities of vengeance and retribution known only in humans. Nonetheless, their strength does appear to be amazing. Live-trapping wolverines for research usually involves building super-strong traps of logs to prevent trapped wolverines from escaping.

Other Names: glutton

Description: Built like stocky marten, low the ground and relatively slim; slender b obscured by heavy winter coat; coat h brown with a light stripe on each side conv ing at base of the tail; head triangular, ho ness above the eyes produces a dark mask; shorter than American marten tail.

Size: Male weight 30 lbs; total length 3-3 tail length 10"; female weight 25 lbs; total ler 2½-3'; tail length 9"

Range: North American range extends ac tundra and south in the Rocky Mountain far as Yellowstone.

Food: Carnivore: in winter mainly carr of winter-killed caribou, moose, white-ta deer; in summer, ptarmigans, ground squirr snowshoe hares, occasional small hooved ma mals such as young caribou.

...ly seen in the North Woods, this female wolverine was photographed on a trail camera ...eff Ford somewhere in the "thumb" of Lower Michigan. Though nicknamed the "Wolverine ...e," there had not been a confirmed sighting in Michigan since the early 1800s. This ...nal roamed the state from 2004 to 2010 when it was found dead, apparently of natural ...ses. Read about this amazing story in *The Lone Wolverine: Tracking Michigan's Most ...ive Animal* (University of Michigan Press, 2012)

...tural History: Wolverines' home ranges are huge, ranging from 40 ...are miles where food is abundant to over 250 square miles where food ...carce. Males' home ranges are much larger than those of females and ...ne ranges of wolverines of the same sex overlap little. Except for the ...eding season and for females raising young, wolverines are solitary.

...male wolverines give birth in late winter in snow caves, in holes under ...ooted trees or in rock dens but always under the snow. Litter size is ...ally 2-3.

...havior: In winter, wolverines travel long distances searching for ...ion.

...wing Tips: Wolverines ...only be seen in the north- ...reaches of our region. If ...learn the location of a ...d deer in the woods, aim ...motely-triggered camera ...he carcass and, if you are ...emely lucky, you might ...a photograph of a wolverine.

American (Pine) Marten *Martes americana*

Old, dense conifer forests with closed canopies and much underbrush. Forage where conifer branches are close to ground.

Nature Notes:

Martens' cream to golden markings on their chins and chests are unique to each marten, allowing individual identification.

Considered "Endangered" by Wisconsin DNR.

A small, introduced population of Eurasian house martens (also called beech or stone martens, *Martes foina*) lives in Wisconsin southwest of Milwaukee. House martens resemble our martens but are usually distinguished easily because the size, color and head shape of the two species differ somewhat. In Wisconsin, the ranges of the two species are well separated and the house martens live outside the range of this field guide.

Other Names: pine marten, marten

Description: Long, slender, and low to ground for its size; smaller than fisher or ho cat, larger than mink and with relatively lor legs than mink; back and head light brown blond; ears pointed and prominent; cream gold markings on chin and chest; tail and dark.

Size: Male weight 1½-3 lbs; total len 1¾-2¼'; tail length 8-10"; female weight lbs; total length 1½-1¾'; tail length 7-8"

Range: Throughout the northern conifer ests of North America except from the Pac Northwest to the Rocky Mountains, wh replaced by the Pacific marten (*Martes cauri*

Food: Carnivore: snowshoe hares, squirr voles and mice, grouse and other birds, eggs chicks, carrion; some fruit in summer.

American marten could be on the trail of Ruffed Grouse, snowshoe hare or red squirrel; ey items important to the marten.

ural History: Males' territories are often 2-3 times larger than those emales. Territories of males do not overlap, nor do territories of ales, but a male's territory will overlap with parts of territories of 2, more females.

April or May, female martens give birth to 1-4 kits, usually 2-3, and lly in a cavity high in a tree but sometimes in hollow logs or in holes er stumps. Martens mate in early autumn. Development of young in uterus is delayed for 8 months so that a female delivers her next litter year after her previous litter. Females first breed when one-year old produce their first litters at age two. Males first breed at age two. ing become independent in autumn.

havior: Martens forage selectively in conifer forests with northern te cedars, eastern hem-ks or balsam firs, forag-under and through low nches and woody debris the ground. They may r a mile or more in a for-ng bout. They walk along tops of logs and sometimes ab trees.

Although martens are extremely agile in trees, and can even jump f tree to tree in some places, they seldom catch red squirrels in t Instead, they catch red squirrels most often when the squirrels are in t middens, which are their underground cone caches.

As is also true for weasels and fishers, martens have high metabolic r Finding enough food to keep warm and to fuel an active lifestyle constant challenge. American martens will sometimes eat pet food outdoors, they will hunt under bird feeders, and sometimes one steal suet put out for birds. Occasionally, a marten will commande hunter's freshly killed deer and defend it as its own.

Viewing Tips: Martens can be bold but generally live away from pec If you learn the location of a dead deer in the woods, aim a remotely gered camera at the carcass and you may get some good marten pho

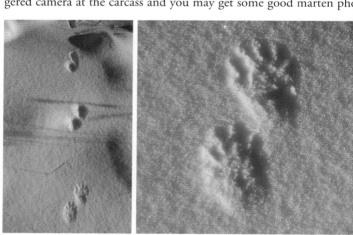

Martens lope in typical weasel fashion with one paw slightly ahead of the other.

This American marten was hot on the trail of this snowshoe hare.

h American martens often kill their own prey, they are not above scavenging on deer
sses or even visiting cabin bird feeders for a suet snack.

ns often rest in trees, in holes, on horizontal limbs (photos left). A marten sitting up
usually looking around; it is more likely "smelling around" and "hearing around." The
is true of all members of the weasel family.

Fisher   *Pekania pennanti*

Forests of deciduous and conifer trees and with an abundance of woo[d] debris and low conifer branches near the ground.

Nature Notes:

The most beautiful mammal in the North Woods, in the authors' humble opinion.

The pattern of white, cream or yellow patches on a fisher's neck, chest and groin are unique and can be used to identify individuals.

Other Names: fisher cat, black cat

Description: Smaller than red fox, larger [than] house cat; long, slender, low to the gro[und;] back and head are brown, tail and legs are g[ray-] black; head has a gold hoary appearance; [ears] are rounded and large but close to the head[.]

Size: Male weight 7-12 lbs; total length [2½-3¼';] tail length 1¼ -1½'; female weight 5-6 lbs; [total] length 2½ -3¼'; tail length 1-1¼'

Range: Throughout the northern forest [of] North America, but not Alaska.

Food: Carnivore: porcupines, snowshoe h[are,] squirrels, grouse, carrion; sometimes mice [and] voles, birds and eggs, lizards and snakes.

Natural History: Female fishers estab[lish] territories of about 6 square miles; males' [ter-] ritories are about 20 square miles but la[rger] where prey are scarce. Territories do not ove[rlap]

...ers may cover a mile or more in hunting forays. They prefer to stick to dense forests.

...ong members of the same sex but do overlap between sexes.

...cats, pumas and coyotes kill and eat fishers, especially in regions that ...e logging, scattered farms, and gravel roads.

...March or April, female fishers give birth to 1-4 kits in a cavity high in ...ee. A week to 10 days after giving birth, females mate. Development ...oung in the uterus is delayed for 10 months, followed by a normal ...gnancy, so a female delivers her next litter one year after her previous ...r. Females first breed when one year old and produce their first lit-...at age two. Males can first breed at age two. Young develop slowly, ...ning their eyes only after about 7 weeks. They become independent ...te autumn.

...avior: Fishers spend most of their time hunting on the ground and ...ping. They may cover a mile or more in a foraging bout. They prefer ...unt in old forests with closed canopies and extensive underbrush ...avoid clearcuts and other open areas. In hardwood forests with ...tered pockets of conifers, ...rs often orient their forag-...towards those pockets. In ...tats where snowshoe hares ...other prey are abundant, ...rs forage in a circuitous ...ion, searching under logs, ...h and low conifer branches. ...y walk along the tops of

Fishers will occasionally visit backyard bird feeding stations.

logs and sometimes climb trees. A fisher can eat an entire snowshoe h
in one sitting if hungry and a snowshoe hare provides a fisher with nu
tion lasting several days.

A fisher kills most prey (but not porcupines) with a bite to the bacl
the neck or head, which kills the prey quickly while protecting the fis
from being bitten. If the fisher is unable to catch a snowshoe hare by
back of the neck or head, it will bite the hare where it can and wrap
supple body around the hare, holding it firmly with all four feet. T
the fisher will redirect its bite to the back of the hare's neck or head
release the foot-hold grip.

Fishers are the only predators specialized to kill porcupines. A fisher
a porcupine with bites to the face, which is the only exposed part of
porcupine not protected by quills. Killing a porcupine is hard work
may require an hour or more, during which time a fisher is consta
trying to keep the porcupine from protecting its face against a tree tr
or rocks. A porcupine provides a fisher with food for a week or mor

**Porcupines have little to fear in the North Woods....except a hungry fisher. A fisher circle
porky (photo left), looking for a chance to attack the face. A fisher may need an hour or
to kill a porcupine.**

cupine in its winter den or up a tree facing away from the trunk is
from a fisher.

wing Tips: Fishers are secretive and most are shy of people. They
most often seen in dense forests with a mix of conifer and deciduous
s. They will come to bait, such as a deer carcass, where they can be
tographed by remote cameras.

gle snowshoe hare can sustain a fisher for several days. Fishers are very tuned in to the
s of the forest. They can vaguely resemble a small fox when loping along and head held
Paired, slightly offset tracks of a fisher in snow.

Short-tailed Weasel (Stoat) *Mustela erminea*

Habitat generalist; hunts for the most common voles and mice in fores
grasslands, and around farmers' fields.

Nature Notes:

Although weasels are usually serious, intensive hunters, when well fed they are delightfully playful. They can nearly turn themselves inside-out with their antics.

Their winter white coat can have a yellowish tinge.

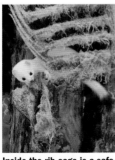

Inside the rib cage is a safe place for an ermine to feed on a dead deer.

Other Names: ermine (a short-tailed we
in white winter coat), stoat (European nam

Description: Long, slender, low to the gro
and small; smaller than an eastern chipmu
males always larger than females; face trian
lar, ears large but rounded, hugging the sl
In summer, body brown with white chin, b
and insides of legs; tail tip black. In winte
the North Woods, white except for black
tip. Short-tailed weasels are smaller than lo
tailed weasels and bigger than least weasels.

Size: Male weight 2-4 oz.; total length 8-
tail length 2½-3½"; female weight 1-3 oz.; t
length 6-10"; tail length 1¾-2½"

Range: Circumpolar; in North America so
from tundra into northern US, further so
in the Midwest and as far south as the ce
Sierra Nevada in California.

f the only animals to change names with the seasons; short-tailed weasels are known as e in winter when their coats turn white.

d: Carnivore: vole specialist but also eats mice, chipmunks, birds, and chicks, other small vertebrates, carrion, in summer some berries.

ural History: Wherever they live, short-tailed weasels are both ators and prey. Predation on weasels by hawks and owls can limit sel populations. The black tip on the tail of a short-tailed weasel can guide an attacking hawk or owl, directing the predator away from body of the weasel towards the tip of the tail. A raptor's talons can grip a weasel's tail, letting the weasel escape.

avior: Specialist predators on voles. The diameter of female short-d weasels matches the diameter of the most common local voles therefore, also matches the size of the voles' tunnels. In the North ods, the most common voles are usually red-backed voles.

most prey with a bite to the back of the neck or head, which dis-hes prey quickly while protecting the weasels from being bitten. If easel is unable to catch its prey by the back of the neck or head, it s the prey wherever it can and wraps its supple body around the prey, ling it firmly with all 4 feet. Then the weasel redirects its bite to the of the neck or head and releases its foot-hold grip.

wing Tips: Catching is hard work, making t-tailed weasels bold and ous about people who are threatening. Remain still n you see a weasel and it come close. Squeaking your lips may bring n even closer.

Minn.
Wisc.
Mich.

Long-tailed Weasel   *Mustela frenata*

Habitat generalist; hunts for the most common voles and mice in [...]
grasslands, and around farmers' fields.

Nature Notes:

Although weasels are usually serious, intensive hunters, when well fed they are delightfully playful. They can nearly turn themselves inside-out with their antics.

A quick squeak can really get the attention of any weasel. They are ever alert for prey. This is a long-tail in its winter white coat. In this stage they are called ermine.

Other Names: ermine (in white wint[...] long-tailed stoat (Europe)

Description: Looks little compared t[...] squirrel; males always larger than [...] Distinguished from least weasel by r[...] large size, long tail with black tip, and [...] to cream belly in summer. Distinguish[...] short-tailed weasel by somewhat larg[...] somewhat longer tail, and yellow to [...] belly in contrast to white belly of sho[...] weasel in summer. In summer, body [...] chin white, underside creamy to yellow [...] black. In winter in the North Wood[...] except for black tail tip. Long-tailed we[...] largest of our three species.

Size: Male weight 6-10 oz.; total lengt[...] tail length 5-6"; female weight 3-9 o[...] length 10-13"; tail length 4-6"

Range: Northern limit is Canada-US [...] range extends into South America.

It's very difficult to identify weasels in the field, especially if you don't see them together. The **whiter throat and belly on this weasel indicates that this is likely a short-tailed weasel.**

Food: Carnivore: voles, mice, birds, eggs and chicks, carrion, berries. Long-tailed weasels kill more large prey, such as chipmunks and young rabbits, than do our other two species of weasels.

Natural History: Territories of a square mile and larger are common; smaller when prey are abundant. Males' territories are large and often encompass the territories of 2-4 females.

Females give birth in April to litters of one to over a dozen young, depending on the abundance of food during pregnancy. They and their female offspring breed in late summer after the young have become independent. When the embryos in their reproductive tracts reach 1-2 weeks of development, they go dormant, delaying implantation until the following March, leading to birth in April.

When prey are abundant during the summer and autumn after they are born, young male long-tailed weasels can grow to be almost twice as heavy as their female counterparts.

Behavior: Females can follow voles down their tunnels and, after dining on a vole, a female often sleeps in its nest. Will follow mice up shrubs and trees and raid birds' nests. All weasels have high metabolic rates and high food require-ments. A female needs to eat at least a vole a day and a male must eat more. If a weasel can kill more than one vole, it will cache those it can not eat immediately to eat later.

Least Weasel *Mustela nivalis (Mustela rixosa)*

Hunts for voles and mice in forests, grasslands, farms and fields.

Nature Notes:

Our smallest carnivore.

A least weasel has a tail so short that having a black tip on it, like weasels of the other two species, would not mis-guide an attacking raptor but would actually guide the raptor to the weasel.

Will cache excess voles when the hunting is good.

May follow mice up shrubs and trees, and raid birds' nests for the eggs.

A species of "Special Concern" in Minnesota.

Other Names: weasel, ermine (occasiona~~ though it lacks a black tail tip)

Description: Smallest of our three weas~ Slender, low to the ground and very small, ~ weigh less than a big vole. In summer, b~ brown with white chin, belly and insides of le~ tail tip may have at most a few black hairs. ~ winter in the North Woods, white.

Size: Male weight 1½-2 oz.; total length 7-~ tail length 1-1½"; female weight 1-1¾ oz.; t~ length 6-7"; tail length ¾-1"

Range: Circumpolar range: in North Amer~ south from tundra into northern US, furt~ south in the Midwest and as far south as ~ southern Appalachian Mountains.

Food: Carnivore: voles and mice, chipmun~ birds, eggs and chicks, other small vertebra~ carrion; in summer some berries.

Natural History: Least weasels breed as ea~ as March and give birth in April. If prey

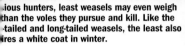
...ious hunters, least weasels may even weigh ...than the voles they pursue and kill. Like the ...-tailed and long-tailed weasels, the least also ...ires a white coat in winter.

...ndant, a female may breed again and have a second litter. If prey ...really abundant, she might even have a third litter. Females born in ...first litter of a year breed at the end of the summer when prey are ...ndant. When lemmings are superabundant in the Arctic, least weasels ...e breed all winter under the snow.

...**havior:** Least weasels spend most of their time foraging or resting. ...ey are so small that they must eat several times a day. If one finds ...lf without food, it must sometimes forage even when most of its prey ...inactive. Least weasels can follow voles down their tunnels and, after ...ing on a vole, a weasel often sleeps in its nest. A least weasel can not ...an entire vole in one sitting, and therefore often has prey cached to ...when hungry.

...**wing Tips:** Every few ...rs when prey are abun- ...t, many young weasels are ...oad, looking for places to ... Often willing to check ...unfamiliar things, weasels ...be curious about people ...o are not threatening.

Minn.

Wisc.

Mich.

American Mink   *Mustela vison*

Minks establish home ranges along waterways in almost any habitat wit abundant prey; sometimes forage far from water.

Nature Notes:

A female will sometimes breed with several males sequentially over a couple weeks. Early-fertilized embryos suspend develop-ment after about 10 days so that all embryos implant in the female's uterus at the same time.

Minks have long been bred and maintained in captivity to harvest their pelts and have been bred for fur colors from white through gray and shades of brown to black. Fur-farm minks that escape survive well in the wild. If you see a mink that is not brown, you know that it or an ancestor had been captive.

Description: Long, slender, and relativ stockier than weasels; about the size of a gray squirrel; males larger than females; u form brown to dark brown except for wh patch under chin and white blotches on n and chest; darker brown than weasels.

Size: Male weight 1½-2½ lbs; total len 1¾-2¼'; tail length 7-9"; female weight 1-2 l total length 1½-2'; tail length 6-7"

Range: Throughout northern North Ameri except the High Arctic, south to northern Gr Plains and to Florida.

Food: Carnivore: muskrats, small mamm sometimes rabbits or hares, birds includ ducks and eggs, also reptiles and amphibia especially frogs, small fish, crayfish.

Natural History: Males' territories can ru half mile or more and usually encompass smaller territories of 2-4 females. Minks'

...s do not hibernate and remain active hunters throughout the harsh northern winters.

...ries extend a couple hundred yards from the water and, in areas with ...tered ponds, lakes and waterways, minks' territories may include large ...s between bodies of water.

...nks breed in spring. Females usually give birth in a den that is a hole ...he ground, often under a root mass near water. Litter size varies but ...sually 3-5. Young are weaned by 6 weeks old.

...havior: Minks often forage along shores, looking into the water from ...truding rocks or trees that have fallen into the water. If a mink sees ...y, it dives into the water to catch it. Minks dive down to 6 feet under ... surface and can stay under water for a minute or more, searching for ...y. They prey on muskrats ...their lodges and will often ...p in the lodges of their ...y.

...wing Tips: Watch any ...reline for a mink. In ...l-summer, you might see a ...ther foraging with her litter.

American Badger   *Taxidea taxus*

Mostly open grassland, meadows, roadsides but sometimes resides in forest.

Nature Notes:

Badgers have been observed, very rarely, hunting cooperatively with coyotes, each appearing to catch more prey than either would hunting alone (photo on opposite page).

During autumn, badgers eat rapaciously to gain fat for the winter. In early winter, they dig a winter den and are largely inactive during the cold. They may come above ground on warm days.

Badgers are equipped with heavy duty claws for digging.

Description: Low to the ground; body bro hoary gray; chest gold to cream; tail sh forepaws broad with long claws; head v central white stripe; white patches below e black stripes in front of white ears. A badg eyes have third eye lids, which protect the e when digging.

Size: Weight 12-25 lbs; total length 2-2¾'; length 4-5"

Range: From Great Lakes states west California, south through central Mexico : north through British Columbia in Canada.

Food: Carnivore: pocket gophers, grou squirrels, small mammals, birds and eggs, r tiles, wasp larvae and pupae.

Natural History: Home ranges vary in : with the abundance of prey and season male home ranges larger than females'. Badg breed in late summer or fall but implantatio

...zingly, coyotes and badgers sometimes hunt cooperatively (like this unlikely duo in North ...ta's Theodore Roosevelt National Park). In this case, the badger digs after prairie dogs ...he coyote stands vigil for any escaping out the "back door."

...yed until February, followed by about ...eeks of pregnancy. Usually 2-3 young ...born in a ground den; eyes open after ...ghly 5 weeks.

...avior: Badgers are largely nocturnal ...ters. Because they are larger than most ...their prey, they cannot pursue prey ...n burrows. Instead, they dig after their ..., excavating prodigious amounts of dirt ...short time. They rest during daytime ...oles dug to catch prey. The holes aerate ...soil and often become dens ...other vertebrates.

...wing Tips: Although ...gers are often considered ...nmals of the prairies, they ...at low densities through- ...the North Woods. They ...most often seen in open ...s.

Otter *Lontra canadensis*

Otters live only in and along shores of wetlands; lakes, streams and rivers. May be seen far from water when traveling overland.

Nature Notes:

Otters forage within complex, 3-dimensional spaces under water, swimming through fallen trees, around underwater boulders, and under overhung banks. They forage in clear calm water, in rapidly flowing water and cloudy, dark water.

Other Names: river otter, northern r otter, American otter

Description: Body tubular, no constrictio neck; tail thick at base and tapered; males ally larger than females; body dark brown variable; ears small; whiskers long and stu feet webbed.

Size: Weight 12-30 lbs; total length 3-4'; length 1-1½'

Range: Originally throughout North Ame except for the desert southwest and Mexico now common mostly in areas with low hur densities.

Food: Carnivore: fish, crayfish, frogs, mu rats, waterbirds and eggs.

Natural History: An otter's home range extend 2-3 miles along lakes, rivers and strea including the Great Lakes. Home ranges

e a quiet backwoods river or lake and you may get a great look at an otter. They are as
s about us as we are about them.

s and females appear to overlap. Otters mark their home ranges with
and urine in places where the scent will be noted by other otters,
as emergent rocks, grassy shoreline and people's docks.

e North Woods, otters appear to breed in late summer or autumn
females exhibit delayed implantation of their embryos. Implantation
rs in mid- to late-winter when days begin to lengthen discernibly.
nale gives birth in a den under roots of fallen trees, in rock crevices,
a den dug by another animal, such as in a beaver's bank den. A
den has an underwater entrance with a bedding area above water
. Litter size is usually 2-3. Young open their eyes after about a month

are weaned by about 3
ths. Young may forage
their mothers for months
being weaned.

avior: Otters forage
r water and have eyes
ted for seeing under water
out distortion. Otters
ar able to use their whis-
to follow the turbulence

Strong social bonds lead to frolicking, wrestling, mutual grooming in pairs or larger grou

trails of fish in cloudy water. Although otters eat any fish they can ca most diet studies show that otters usually catch more slow, non-g fish than fast-swimming fish. Given that otters are usually found at l densities on North Woods lakes than fishermen, most otters lose n fish to fishermen than fishermen lose fish to otters.

Otters often live in social groups, usually comprising a female and most recent young and sometimes an adult male. Otters slide down or snow into water and appear excited about play. Social groups so times wrestle.

In winter, otter tracks in the snow show a belly drag and show w otters glide downhill on the snow (photo opposite page). Otters so times travel long distances on land going from one waterway to ano

Viewing Tips: Get up early and canoe or kayak a quiet river or shore. Look along water courses and shoreline for otters' feces. Fece filled with fish scales and crushed crayfish shells that become bleac In waterways that have otter latrines, watch for the otters whenever are near or on the water.

...np" of otters. Otters often live in social groups made up of a female and her last brood ...s.

...tter (above left) has made a meal of a large frog. Classic "lope, lope, glide" tracks of ...er traveling overland in winter. This is an efficient method of locomotion and they can ...imes slide many feet on their bellies, much longer slides have been recorded on slight ...ill slopes. Otters may travel overland far from open water.

...called "river otter," but this species does not discriminate between aquatic habitats. ...two are living quite happily in Lake Superior.

Northern Raccoon   *Procyon lotor*

Raccoons are habitat generalists that live in forests, farm land, and cities with trees.

Nature Notes:

The raccoon's scientific name means "pre-dog that washes." Although raccoons do not wash their food, they often forage for food in shallow water by moving their forepaws along the bottom, feeling for crayfish or mussels.

Rabies causes infrequent epizootics in raccoon populations. Be aware of such epizootics and avoid raccoons that exhibit odd behavior, such as being friendly towards humans.

Raccoon track in mud. Note the long, finger-like print.

Description: Eminently recognizable masked face and ringed tail; stout body gri brown, gray or reddish; black mask across with white patches above and below eyes distinctly ringed in brown and black.

Size: Weight 4-20 lbs; total length 2-3'; length 8-15"

Range: Found throughout the United S except the desert Southwest, into sout Canada and throughout Central America South America.

Food: Omnivore: crayfish, mussels, small also small mammals, birds, eggs (of birds turtles), fruits, grains, human garden prod

Natural History: Home ranges overlap and usually oriented around water. Wolves coyotes sometimes prey on raccoons.

Raccoons breed in mid- to late winter and

Though often maligned for their behavior, raccoons are really beautiful animals.

...n to litters averaging around 4 kits about 9 weeks later. Lactation lasts ...ut 10 weeks and youngsters begin foraging on their own when 4-5 ...ths old. Although young raccoons are extremely cute, they grow up ...e mammals that behave completely differently from dogs and cats. ...s, their behavior can be unpredictable and they make very poor pets.

...avior: Raccoons forage extensively around and in water, where they ...in much of their food. Nonetheless, they can forage far from water ...are pleased to raid gardens, where they can eat prodigious amounts ...markably short times. Because raccoons are agile climbers, fences do ...deter them.

...wing Tips: Raccoons are ...n seen at night, often in ...headlights of cars. They ...n visit bird feeders, espe-...y platform feeders, at ...t.

Black Bear   *Ursus americanus*

Areas that are forested or that have at least many scattered woodlots. Black bears generally avoid areas with high human densities.

Nature Notes:

Black bears have prehensile lips that are perfect for picking berries without collecting leaves and raw fruits (see photo above of bear plucking individual rose hips with its lips).

Bears disperse seeds, spreading blueberry, raspberry, saskatoon and pin cherry seeds across the landscape. Although most berry seeds do not need to pass through a mammal's or bird's digestive tract to be able to germinate, seeds in bear scats are planted with abundant fertilizer and grow well.

Other Names: North American black b[ear,] North American bear, bear

Description: Large, stocky mammals; b[ody] usually uniform black but color morphs inc[lude] brown, gray, cream and white; tail short; [legs] sturdy. In North Woods, brown black b[ears] seen occasionally; brown-colored black b[ears] are not to be confused with brown (also ca[lled] grizzly) bears, which are found elsewher[e in] North America but not in the North Woo[ds.]

Size: Male weight 100-500 lbs; total le[ngth] 4-6'; tail length 3-6"; female weight 80-300[lbs;] total length 4-5'; tail length 3-6"

Range: Originally found throughout N[orth] America but now restricted mostly to fore[sted] areas across the boreal forests of Canada, d[own] the Appalachian Mountains, down the R[ocky] Mountains into Mexico and down the Cas[cade] Mountains and Sierra Nevada.

cubs climb a near tree, often a white pine, oak, aspen or big white cedar, when mom
her order. This is a crucial safety behavior as male bears will kill cubs.

d: Omnivore: in spring green vegetation, fawns of white-tailed deer;
immer berries and fruits; in autumn apples, late berries, hazelnuts
acorns; throughout mild seasons larvae and pupae of ants, bees and
s. Will raid bird feeders, garbage cans, gardens and bee hives.

ural History: Black bears' lives in the North Woods are dominated
ie annual disappearance of almost all food at the beginning of win-
From the time spring foods become available until the last acorns
hazelnuts are gone, bears eat to gain weight to survive the next
er. Gaining 100-200 pounds during the active season is not uncom-
. When winter comes, black bears head into dens. Common den
s include a hole under a root mass, a hole in a bank, a bear-sized,
y cave, a nest under thick
tation or under the stars, a
in a tree, or a comfy place
r a family's porch or deck.
ing winter, black bears do
eat, drink, urinate or defe-
and can lose all the weight
gained. Come spring, the
ess starts again.

Minn.

Wisc.

Mich.

Black bear sign: track in soft soil and a northern white cedar clawed by a bear.

Female black bears give birth to cubs in their winter dens, around the [...] of January. Newborn cubs, usually 2-3 in a litter, are small, nearly n[...] and weigh only ½-1 pound. They nurse all winter, often between a [...] and a soft place, and grow while their mother snoozes, cleans them, [...] as they get older, plays with them. When cubs and mother leave thei[...]

in spring, cubs are ready to start e[...] soft foods, like ant larvae and pu[...]

Cubs stay with their mothers thr[...] the next winter and begin liv[...] their own during spring when [...] are over one year old. Their mo[...] breed that spring or early sum[...] and embryos delay implantation [...] early winter, leading to gestation [...] lasts only about two months. He[...] female black bears produce cubs [...] other year.

Bear den in the upturned base of a fallen tree.

Females defend territories in [...] North Woods but have overlap[...] home ranges in other parts of their range where food is more abun[...] Home ranges or territories are usually 5 to 15 square miles for fem[...] Territories of males are larger than those of females and territories o[...] really big males that do most of the breeding can be 5 times larger [...] females' territories.

Behavior: During spring, females with cubs tend not to travel fa[...] to stay near good food. Mothers keep close track of their cubs and r[...]

to three cubs is an average litter for a female black bear; rarely does a female have four s.

m several times a day. Females ready to breed will travel long disces, advertising to male bears. Some females breed with two or more les and can produce litters with more than one father.

ewing Tips: Once a bear learns a source of food, it will return. Bee es and gardens often require electric fences to be safe. Bird feeders ist be moved to places where bears can not reach them and be mounted h very sturdy wires or posts. Most black bears prefer to avoid people l run when confronted with a person swinging his or her arms and ing. Consider yourself fortunate to see a black bear in the wild.

rs sometimes come into northern towns to fatten up for winter. When they do, they often ict a crowd of onlookers. Cubs go up and down trees on command of their mother.

Lynx   *Lynx canadensis*

Boreal forests, especially with low conifer branches or alder bogs and other places with high densities of snowshoe hares.

Nature Notes:

Lynxes are protected in the United States with threatened status under the Endangered Species Act. Lynx populations are not endangered or threatened in Canada.

Other Names: wildcat, Canada lynx

Description: Distinctly bigger than dome cat; usually appears bigger than bobcat due long legs though they may weigh less; body g to cream, sometimes pale reddish brown, w dark spots; winter coat lush, thick, usually lig er than summer coat; cheek tufts; ears bl with tufts on tips; backs of ears have promin white spot; tail shorter than bobcat with fully capped with black; feet larger than pur

Size: Weight 15-35 lbs; total length 2-3½'; length 4-5"

Range: Boreal forests of Canada and so into northern Minnesota, Wisconsin, UP Michigan, and into the western mountains.

Food: Carnivore: specialists on snowshoe ha (80% of diet), also squirrels, mice and vo beavers, birds and eggs, rarely small deer. V eat carrion.

the huge paws of the lynx; these oversized feet serve as "snowshoes" for efficient travel hunting in deep snow.

ural History: Lynx's home ranges are usually 10 square miles or er. Males' home ranges are generally larger than females' and home ges overlap, especially those of females. Lynx populations rise and in size with the 10-year cycle of snowshoe hare populations. Because wshoe hare cycles have become less pronounced in the North Woods, Lynx population cycles have become less pronounced here as well.

snowshoe hare-lynx population cycle is the result of hares overeat- their food supply when their population is high. At that stage of cycle, the lynx population is growing because lynxes have lots of s to eat. As the hare population decreases because of lack of food, es search diligently for the reasing numbers of hares, ressing the hare population further. Then the lynx ulation crashes because of of food, by which time d for hares is recovering, wing the hare population ebuild.

Minn.

Wisc.

Mich.

Lynxes breed in late winter usually, producing litters of 2-4 kittens so 9-10 weeks later. The natal den is usually a hollow log, a hole under a r mass or a similar site. Kittens' eyes open at about 10 days of age and t are weaned by two months. Kittens may stay with their mother until next breeding season.

Behavior: Lynxes often crouch and wait for snowshoe hares, attack with a short rush. Their big feet keep them from sinking deep into sn Lynxes are less skittish than bobcats and often linger when observed a person.

Viewing Tips: Driving remote forest roads early in the morning areas with known snowshoe hare populations) may eventually yiel glimpse of a lynx. Fortunately, they can be quite tame once spott allowing for a lingering look. Sometimes are attracted to carrion, so s ting a camera on a deer carcass in the woods could yield photos of a ly

Lynx family on a quiet North Woods backroad. Three kits is quite average with a range of t to four per litter.

er and kitten out and about on a summer morning. Note that the tip of the tail is com-
y black; bobcats show only black on the top of the tail.

s can appear much larger than bobcats due to their enormous paws, long legs and
winter coats. Also note the lynx's long ear tufts; bobcats' ear tufts are shorter. Although
s are up to 6-times heavier than lynxes, lynx tracks are often larger than puma tracks.

Bobcat *Lynx rufus*

Diverse habitats—farmland to dense forests. Highest densities in areas with woodlots scattered within open farmland.

Nature Notes:

Bobcats and lynxes hybridize occasionally and hybrids are difficult to identify. Finding a cat with a very short tail but with a white underside, or a cat with a longer tail but black all around the tip probably indicates a hybrid.

Bobcat approaching deer carcass.

Other Names: wildcat

Description: Bigger than domestic cat; b reddish brown, sometimes creamy or c brown, usually with dark spots; tail short longer than lynx with black tip that is w underneath; cheek tufts; ears tipped with s tufts; backs of ears have prominent white s Bobcats usually look smaller than lynxes tho they may weigh more.

Size: Weight 10-30 lbs; total length 2-4'; length 5-7"

Range: Throughout the United States, ac extreme southern Canada and much of Mex

Food: Carnivore: rabbits, squirrels, turk mice and voles, birds and eggs; rarely s deer. Will eat carrion, such as road-killed d

Natural History: Bobcat home ranges usually 10 square miles or larger. Males' h ranges are generally larger than females'

...ats seem to be increasing in the North Woods in recent decades. This may be due to a ...ination of habitat, prey and climate changes.

...e ranges overlap little within each sex. Bobcats are the only spotted ...in the world whose populations are not so limited that they deserve ...tection. In recent decades, bobcats have been extending their range ...h into territory formally occupied only by lynxes.

...oss their range, bobcats have been documented giving birth to kittens ...l times of year, even in the dead of winter in places that are cold. In ...North Woods, they breed in spring usually, producing litters of 3-5 ...ens. Kittens' eyes open at about 10 days of age and kittens are weaned ...wo months. Kittens start foraging some on their own when around ...months of age and are mostly on their own by seven months.

...**avior:** Bobcats can be active any time of the day. They hunt singly. ...ere they live near people, ...y often avoid daytime activ- ...They often crouch and ...t for prey, attacking with a ...rt rush.

...**wing Tips:** Bobcats are ...erally more secretive than ...xes, giving only fleeting ...npses.

Puma (Mountain Lion/Cougar) *Puma concolo*

Although not limited to forests, pumas are generally found where trees exist.

Nature Notes:

Pumas often travel 5-10 miles a night, hunting, usually in 1-2 hour bouts.

Pumas are never black.

Dispersing juvenile males tend to wander farther looking for a place to settle down than do juvenile females. The transient pumas in the North Woods are predominantly juvenile males. They travel long distances and never settle in one place for long. A puma seen in Minnesota in June could be in Wisconsin in July and New York in August.

Other Names: mountain lion, cougar, c mount, panther

Description: Big cat, almost 3 feet tall at shoulders; tawny brown except for white pa at tip of muzzle; tail long, slender. Kitt brown to gray with spots.

Size: Weight 75-200 lbs; total length 5-8'; length 2-3'

Range: Originally throughout the Amer from Alaska to Tierra del Fuego but range North America now only west of the Bl Hills in South Dakota and an isolated popu tion in southern Florida. No resident popu tion in North Woods but occasional transi individuals.

Food: Carnivore: large, wild hooved ma mals predominantly (white-tailed deer North Woods), occasionally livestock. Will carrion.

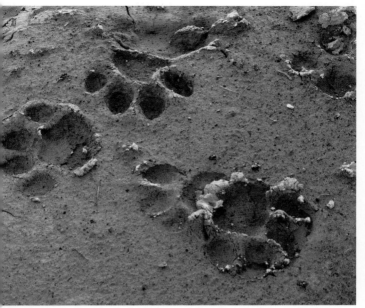

...arge round tracks of a puma in riverbottom mud. Note the lack of claw marks; Cats can
...ct their claws, dogs cannot.

...ural History: Where pumas are resident they have large home
...es, often 100 square miles or more.

...orthern areas, pumas most often breed in spring and give birth about
...onths later. Kittens stay with their mothers for as long as 1-2 years. No
...rs have been documented from resident females in the North Woods.

...avior: In the North Woods, pumas are generally active at night.
...es and females hunt singly. Pumas stalk prey mostly on the ground,
...ing with a rush. Although attacks from elevated positions, such as
...n a tree or rock, have been reported, they appear to be rare. A puma
...stay near a kill for a few days, usually sharing the kill with scavengers.

...puma will usually cover
...kill with leaves and dirt
...rest some distance away.

...wing Tips: Pumas do eat
...ion so a remote camera set
...a deer carcass just might
...d a photo of a puma.

Wapiti (Elk) *Cervus canadensis*

Wapiti prefer open habitats associated with shrubs, especially willows, and that are near forest.

Nature Notes:

A big bull wapiti's antlers can weigh as much as 35 pounds.

Bull wapiti begin growing antlers in May; they are fully developed by late August in time for the fall rut. Males shed antlers by March or April with big, healthy bulls shedding theirs first.

Antler rub in fall.

Other Names: elk, North American *Cervus elaphus* is former scientific name.

Description: Not as large as moose but inctly bigger than white-tailed deer. Body brown, sometimes light red-brown; dark br mane and face; light-colored rump patch rounding a short tail. Calves' coats have w spots; they lose their spots when they shed i their winter coats in late autumn. Antlers re distinctly back, then up, featuring a main with upward facing smaller tines and someti a fork near the tip.

Size: Male (bull) weight 375-1050 lbs; t length 7-8'; tail length 4-7"; female (cow) we 375-650 lbs; total length 6-8'; tail length 3-7

Range: Distribution circumpolar if wa and Eurasian red deer are the same spe Before European settlement of North Amer range extended from what is now the wes

wapiti guards his harem of cows in late fall. He will breed with several during the rut.

nd Canada in the Rocky Mountains eastward as far as the southern
lachians; now limited mainly to western US.

d: Herbivore: grasses and herbaceous vegetation in spring; leaves of
os and saplings in summer; buds and small branches in winter.

ral History: Wolves are the major predators of wapiti in Ontario.
althy, adult wapiti can usually outrun or defend itself against wolves.
sequently, wolves generally kill old, injured or sick wapiti. The major
es of mortality in Michigan are legal and illegal hunting.

iti breed in late autumn and give birth in early June, usually to a
e calf. Calves stand and nurse within 1½ hours. Calves are indepen-
by autumn but female calves often remain associated with their
ers. Healthy yearling females will breed.

avior: During the breeding season, males guard small herds of
les (harems) that are entering breeding condition. Males advertise
presence, dominance and guarding of females by "bugling," a shrill
le-like sound. Males fight over possession of females, intertwining
antlers, pushing and shoving.

ving Tips: Minnesota
lation centered around
la; Michigan herds
Gaylord and Wolverine
gle "elk viewing brochure").
act the state DNRs
e Ontario Ministry of
ral Resources for specific
ions of their wapiti herds.

White-tailed Deer *Odocoileus virginianus*

Best habitat is a mix of open land, open forest, scattered woodlots and some farm land with roughly 50 percent forested.

Nature Notes:

Deer drop their tails, hiding the white flag, when they leave an open area and enter forest. They also stop running and stand stock still just inside the forest, partially hidden by brush. Without the obvious tail flag, they disappear from view.

Other Names: deer, whitetail

Description: Large mammal; males (bu larger than females (does), males standing u 4½ feet at the shoulder. Body brown, more brown in summer and gray-brown in wi large black nose; prominent brown ears; eye to the sides of the head; neck often with w bib; tail large, white underneath. Fawns' have white spots; they lose their spots w they shed into their winter coats in autu Each antler has a main tine that rises and bends distinctly forward with smaller aimed upward; in contrast, antlers of wapit much larger and reach back.

Size: Male weight 100-300 lbs; total le 5-7'; tail length 10-14"; female weight 75-25(total length 4-6'; tail length 10-14"

Range: From the southern boreal fores Canada south throughout the US, Mexico South America.

shed their antlers in winter; often losing one antler before the other.

d: Herbivore: Mainly browser but will graze and will eat row crops as corn and soybeans. In summer, in addition to leaves of shrubs rees, aquatic vegetation in shallow water. In winter, buds and small ches of deciduous shrubs and trees, also buds, small branches and les of nutritious conifers, especially white cedar and white pine.

ral History: Wolves are the major predators on white-tailed deer e North Woods after humans, who kill more deer during an autumn ing season than wolves kill all year. Healthy deer can usually outrun ght off attacking wolves. Coyotes, domestic dogs, pumas and occa-lly bobcats also kill deer in smaller numbers. Black bears prey upon y-dropped fawns in spring.

can reach high densities in areas with abundant food, upwards o per square mile. The average litter size for deer in an area also cts the quality and abundance of food. Where food is abundant, y deer have triplets; where food is scarce, singletons are the norm.

1s nurse immediately after
and walk within hours.
hers leave young fawns
ed and hiding while they
ge, returning to nurse
young 3-4 times a day.
couple weeks old, fawns
to browse, by which time
have doubled their birth
ht. Female fawns in very

The spotted coat of a fawn is great camouflage for a sun-dappled forest floor.

good condition can breed in autumn and produce fawns on their first birthdays. Most females breed for the first time as yearlings.

Behavior: During the breeding season, bucks thrash saplings with antlers and leave scent marks. These "rubs" signal to other males ar does. A buck usually guards a doe or a small group of does when the becoming receptive to breeding. Bucks will fight over possession of

In winter where snow becomes deep, deer gather in traditional pl called "yards," usually with dense conifer cover. Some deer migrate distances in autumn and spring to and from yards. Yards tend t located on the boundaries of wolf packs' territories, where wolves s little time.

When deer are startled or flee from predators, they often bound and lift their tails, showing the prominent white patch underneath. flagging signals to other deer but no one knows exactly what the s means. Many suggestions have been tested but always with equiv results. Flagging tails allow deer to keep track of group mates, allow to follow a group member in the lead and tell a predator that it has detected and will not be able to catch the deer. Fawns flag more adults do.

Viewing Tips: White-tailed deer often graze on roadside grass ir evening or early morning, especially in spring and autumn when g grass is at a premium. Also look for deer in open pastures. In sum look for whitetails foraging on aquatic plants in shallow water, eve mid-day.

ng from perceived or real danger, a white-tailed deer flashes its white undertail.

Moose   *Alces alces*

Moose prefer cool forests interspersed with openings and water.

Nature Notes:

Largest mammal in the North Woods.

Antlers of a big male moose can weigh as much as 80 pounds.

It's time to move on when a moose has its ears back.

Other Names: elg or elk (in Scandinavia)

Description: Big; males (bulls) up to 6 tall at shoulders, larger than female (cow). B brown, often black on the neck; tops of legs belly; head large with large ears, bulbous n chin of male has prominent "beard;" ant palmate and up to 6 feet across.

Size: Male weight 800-1300 lbs; total len 8-10½'; tail length 3-5"; female weight 600- lbs; total length 7½-10'; tail length 3-5'

Range: Distribution circumpolar (Scandina Russia); in North America in the boreal for from Alaska to Labrador, including the for down the Rocky Mountains to Yellowstone

Food: Herbivore: mainly browser; in sumn leaves of shrubs and trees, aquatic vegetat in shallow water; in winter, buds and sr branches of deciduous shrubs and trees, es cially willows, also buds, small branches needles of nutritious conifers, especially bal

Bulls take a break from sparring during the October rut (top). Moose are adapted to deep ; they have shoulder joints that allow them to lift their legs higher than their bellies. e calf; twins are the norm for healthy cows.

nd white pine. May eat up to 50 pounds of twigs a day in winter.

ural History: Home ranges can be as small as a couple square miles. g legs allow moose to travel through snow in winter and their long and long skulls allow them to forage on aquatic plants in water nearly eep as moose are tall. Moose are prey for wolves but a healthy, adult se can defend itself successfully with well-placed kicks. Cow moose nd their calves formidably. Where alternate prey, such as white-tailed , are available, wolves often favor those prey over moose.

lers begin growing on males in spring and reach their full size by early mn. During the breeding season, bulls thrash saplings with their ers and leave scent marks. These "rubs" signal to other bulls and to s that a healthy, adult male earby and ready to breed. ull usually guards a cow n she is becoming recep- to breeding. Bulls drop r antlers after the breeding on and most big bulls have their antlers by the turn of new year. Young bulls in elor groups practice spar-

ring during autumn and may retain their antlers a bit longer than ~~large bulls.

Cow moose give birth in late May to early June after an 8 month gesta tion. Births are synchronous within a couple days for all female moose a population. In the few days before giving birth, expectant mothers oft wander long distances with unpredictable changes in direction. The movements are believed to elude predators. Cows in good conditi often give birth to twins, otherwise litter size is one. Calves usually sta and nurse within 1½ hours. They weigh 25-30 pounds or more at bir and gain 2-2½ pounds a day while nursing. Mothers stay close to th calves and usually stay near the birth site for a few weeks. Young becor independent before their mothers give birth to their next young. Bc males and females reach their peak reproductive years when about age

Behavior: Moose avoid foraging on land during hot summer days. ~~ avoid heat, they rest in cool, shaded areas or forage for aquatic plar Aquatic plants are higher in sodium, a limiting mineral for moose, th are leaves of terrestrial plants. Aquatic plants, however, contain mu

Moose have large splayed hooves that help them traverse wet and mucky ground. Inch-lon droppings are often called "moose marbles." Shed antlers rarely survive long enough to host lichens; they are usually gnawed into oblivion by small rodents seeking a calcium fix. moose-thrashed balsam fir is a rub made by a bull's antlers; he also left scent marks here

er and fill a moose's rumen faster than do leaves of terrestrial plants, ing moose to stop foraging sooner. As a result, moose must balance r sodium requirements against their total nutritional requirements forage both in the water and on land.

wing Tips: Moose are often observed foraging on aquatic plants or water in summer. If on a canoe trip in moose country, get up early go for a dawn paddle to increase your chances.

atic plants can be 10 times higher in sodium than land plants. It's no wonder moose often can een foraging in bogs, marshes and lakes. Swimming also provides relief from biting insects.

va Indian hunters historically used birchbark megaphones to project their imitations of the cow to lure in bulls during the rut. Moderns hunters and photographers continue this tradition.

Woodland Caribou *Rangifer tarandus*

In the North Woods, caribou live only in boreal forest.

Nature Notes:

Antler growth by females may have evolved in response to the need to defend winter foraging sites.

Our "woodland" caribou is the same species as the migrating "barren ground" caribou of Alaska and Canada's tundra, and the reindeer of Scandinavia and Siberia.

The last confirmed sighting of caribou south of the Canadian border in our region was a pair that wintered over in the Hovland, Minnesota area in 1980-81. The pair likely wandered south from a northwest Ontario population.

Reindeer lichens (*Cladina*) are a critical winter food.

Other Names: caribou, reindeer (Scandinav…

Description: Smaller than moose and wap… but larger than white-tailed deer; males larg… than females. Coat pale brown to gray, oft… with a pale mane; face is shorter than … moose. Both males and females grow antle… males' antlers are larger; antlers usually have palmate brow tine and a main tine that stretc… es back, up and then forward with branchi… tines that mostly face up; antlers of wapiti a… deer are not palmate at all; antlers of moose … broadly palmate.

Size: Male weight 175-325 lbs; total leng… 5½-7'; tail length 4-9"; female weight 150-2… lbs; total length 5-6'; tail length 4-8"

Range: Boreal forests and tundra across nor… ern North America and Eurasia.

Food: Herbivore: grasses and succulent lea… from shrubs, especially willow; lichens in wint…

cows (pictured) and bulls grow antlers over the summer. The antlers are shed in winter.
...da has highlighted the caribou on its quarter coin.

...tural History: Our woodland caribou do not migrate, in contrast to ...se on the tundra. Wolves are their major predators. Caribou breed in ... autumn and early winter and give birth to single calves in late May ...arly June. Calves nurse and follow their mothers a few hours after ...h. Calves nurse until winter but depend mostly on forage for food ...r reaching about 1½ months of age.

...havior: Males fight for access to females during the relatively short ...ding season and lose body reserves, leaving them to play catch-up ...winter.

...ring winter, caribou eat mostly terrestrial lichens and must dig for ...n as snow grows deep. Digging uses considerable energy so caribou ...rd and defend their foraging sites. Good foraging sites are very valu-...e, because when a foraging site becomes depleted, the energetic cost ...finding another foraging ...is great.

...wing Tips: Kayaking Lake ...erior's Slate Islands may be ...r best bet to see one in the ...rth Woods. Contact the ...tario Ministry of Natural ...ources for specific locations ...caribou populations.

Red Bat *Lasiurus borealis*

Edge habitats next to water, open fields, farmland, urban areas.

Nature Notes:

Red bats often begin foraging 1-2 hours after sunset, later than most other bats. They forage sometimes for insects on the ground.

Mostly solitary and roost during the day on trees and shrubs, sometimes near the ground. Some migrate, apparently in groups, and the two sexes migrate at different times and to different places.

Description: Back and face red; ears relative short and rounded; tail long; males brigh than females. Strong fliers.

Size: Weight ¼-½ oz.; total length 4½"; t length 1½"

Range: Most of the US except the Roc Mountains.

Food: Insectivore: moths, flies, beetles, crick and cicadas.

Natural History: Red bats breed in ea autumn and give birth in June to 1-5 ti naked young that cling to their mothers' f A mother leaves her young to fora Young can fly and are wean when about a month old.

Minn.

Wisc.

Mich.

ary Bat *Lasiurus cinereus*

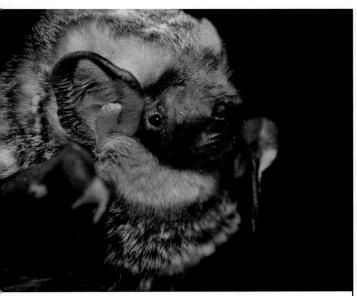

ary bats are found in all habitats, tundra to southern forests.

scription: Relatively large; fur brown to
with white-tipped hairs; ears relatively
t and rounded; females larger than males.
ngest, swiftest fliers in the North Woods.

e: Weight 1 oz.; total length 6"; tail
th 2"

ge: Most of North America except Alaska
northwest Canada.

d: Insectivore: prefer moths but also flies,
les, grasshopper, dragonflies, wasps.

ural History: Females
birth to 1-4 pups covered
fine, silver fur. Young
g to their mother's fur but
g from a twig or leaf while
r mother forages. Ears
n by 3 days after birth,
by 12 days, and by a little
a month, young can fly.

Nature Notes:

Hoary bats are solitary and
roost during the day in foliage 15-30 feet above the
ground, often visible from
the ground.

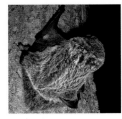

Minn.

Wisc.

Mich.

Silver-haired Bat   *Lasionycteris noctovagans*

Grassland areas and forests, including old growth forests.

Nature Notes:

Silver-haired bats begin foraging shortly after sunset and forage at tree-top level in wooded areas and above ponds and streams. They prey mostly on flying insects.

In summer, silver-haired bats roost during the day, either singly or in small groups, in hollow trees, tree cavities, under exfoliating bark.

Description: Dark brown to black coa_ silver-tipped guard hairs on back ar front half of the tail membrane; ears sm rounded. Smaller than a hoary bat.

Size: Weight ¼-½ oz.; total length ⸗ length 1½"

Range: Throughout most of the US exc⸗ extreme southeast and southwest.

Food: Insectivore: mostly moths but als⸗ beetles, leafhoppers, bugs, midges and fli⸗

Natural History: Females often form n colonies where litters of 1-2 pups ar in June. Pups are weaned by a month of age.

Minn.

Wisc.

Mich.

icolored Bat (Pipistrelle)   *Perimyotis subflavus*

age over open pasture and adjacent to vegetation.

er Names: pipistrelle, eastern pipistrelle, colored bat. Formerly *Pipistrellus subflavus.*

scription: Small. Body yellow-brown to -brown. Weak, fluttering flight.

e: Weight ¼ oz.; total length 3"; tail length 1¼"

age: Eastern half of the US through east tal Mexico further south.

od: Insectivore: moths, beetles, leafhoppers, ; mostly small insects.

ural History: In summer, maternal colo- can be in attics, barns hollow trees. Individuals st under leaves. Tricolored mate in autumn and give h to twin pups in June. s at birth weigh about a a as much as their moth- They can fly by 2-3 weeks ge. Hibernate alone or in ll dense clusters deep in s or mines.

Nature Notes:

In January 1990, Bruce "Bunter" Knowles discovered a hibernating Tricolored Bat in a cave at the base of Palisade Head, a 300' cliff on Minnesota's North Shore of Lake Superior. This represented a 200 mile northerly range extension for a hibernation location for this species.

Considered "Threatened" in Wisconsin and "Special Concern" in Minnesota.

Little Brown Bat *Myotis lucifugus*

These bats often forage over water and near water in forests.

Nature Notes:

A delightful and tiny bat.

Many populations decreased due to White-nose Syndrome.

Female little brown bats return to the same nursery each year.

Do not use bat houses extensively.

Other Names: little brown myotis

Description: Distinctly small, brown perhaps nondescript. Flight often with tw and turns.

Size: Weight ¼ oz.; total length 3"; tail ler 1½"

Range: Widespread across forested N America

Food: Insectivore: caddisflies, mayflies midges, some mosquitoes.

Natural History: Some little brown migrate hundreds of miles between their s mer foraging sites and their hibernating s They hibernate in underground caves and mines. They mate in late summer and fen give birth to single pups in a colonial roost about two months after leaving hibernat At birth, pups weigh about a quarter of mother's weight. Females leave pups in the ony site while foraging, finding their own p

ears aid in echolocation of prey; they can determine size and speed of prey, and pinpoint ation. Contrary to popular belief, they have good vision, which can also aid in hunting.

eturn from their calls and odors. Pups ingest only milk for about 2½ s, by which time they begin foraging on their own.

avior: A little brown bat often catches insects by curling its tail and legs forward, forming a basket with its tail membrane. It then curls dy to grab the insect with its mouth, all done on the fly.

wing Tips: For the supreme bat viewing experience, explore lakes streams in a canoe during late dusk in summer. You will know when have found a favorite foraging site because hundreds of bats will fly and around you, between you and your canoe partners. You will hear chirps as the bats communicate with each other and you will hear muffled wing beats. The experience is awesome.

Northern Long-eared Bat *Myotis septentrion*

Summer roosts in live trees and snags, under bark and in cavities or in colonies. Rarely in manmade structures.

Nature Notes:

Federally listed as a Threatened species.

These bats glean insects, often large insects, from the ground, branches and foliage. They will fly with big insects to perches to eat. They key into prey by listening for moving or flying insects.

Hibernate in caves and mines, often with the more common little brown bats.

Other Names: northern long-eared long-eared bat, long-eared myotis

Description: Small brown bat wi sharply pointed ears and a long tragu guished from little brown bat by its l Flies close to branches and foliage.

Size: Weight ¼ oz.; total length 3"; ta 1¼"

Range: From the southern App Mountains north through the souther forests of Canada.

Food: Insectivore: often eats larg

Natural History: Fem: a single pup in spring reproductive cycle is similar to that of littl bats.

Minn.

Wisc.

Mich.

g Brown Bat *Eptesicus fuscus*

age over rivers, along forest-field edges, above agricultural crops and ng city streets.

cription: A big, brown bat with black, d wings and a dark mask. Strong, fast t.

e: Weight ¾ oz.; total length 4½"; tail th 1¾"

ge: Found from the southern boreal for- of Canada throughout the US, through ico and further south.

d: Insectivore: has a preference for beetles.

ural History: Mate in early autumn and birth to twins in early mer. Maternal colonies be in hollow trees, attics alls of houses, barns or ches. Females leave young rage. Young can fly by month of age.

Nature Notes:

Often seen foraging in cities.

Can fly up to 20 miles per hour and catch an insect every 3 seconds. A lactating female can eat nearly her own weight in insects each night.

Nocturnal. Leave day roosts some 20 minutes after sunset and forage for 1 to 2 hours.

Considered "Threatened" in Wisconsin.

Snowshoe Hare   *Lepus americanus*

Snowshoe hares favor forests with complex structure near the ground, including logs, brush and low conifer branches.

Nature Notes:

Molt by snowshoe hares is triggered by changing day length and not by snowfall.

Snowshoe hares need a month to molt, and day length is a better predictor of the average snow conditions than is snow cover, which can change over short periods.

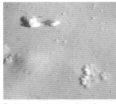

Bobcat and snowshoe hare tracks in a bog.

Other Names: snowshoe rabbit, varying h

Description: Medium-sized hare. Du summer, body brown with gray chin and b tail top brown, bottom white; body whit winter, ears with black tips.

Size: Weight 2-3 lbs; total length 15-20"; length 1-2"

Range: Throughout the boreal forests North America, extending south into the at high elevations in the western mountain: the Appalachians, and around the Great La

Food: Herbivore: in summer, grasses, he ceous vegetation, leaves of low shrubs and lings; in winter, inner bark and buds of sh and saplings including young tamaracks.

Natural History: Snowshoe hares start br ing in late winter and can produce 2-5 li before late summer. Litter size varies from 8, depending on time of year and a mot

Summer-pelaged snowshoe hare deep in a northern black spruce bog. Shortening days in fall trigger their slow change to white fur.

...dition. Leverets are born fully furred with eyes and ears open and can ... if surprised by predators. Mothers leave their young in safe, protected ...es and return periodically to nurse them.

...wshoe hares are the drivers of the 10-year population cycles of many ...nals and plants in the boreal forests. When the hare population is ... winter food plants grow, sprouting new, low branches and send-...up new seedlings and saplings. Because little of this new growth ...rowsed by hares, plants do not protect the new growth with repel-...compounds. With abundant food, the snowshoe hare population ...ws and, after a few years, ...ns to overeat its food sup-...Heavy browsing by hares ...ow branches of shrubs and ...ings, especially willows and ...ns, causes plants to pro-...regrowing branches with ...pounds that inhibit diges-...by hares, making good ...scarce. At the same time,

predator populations grow in response to the growing hare pop[ula]tion, especially the lynx population but also fisher, marten, North[ern] Goshawk, and Great Horned Owl populations. The hare popula[tion] begins to decrease because of food shortage, causing predators to se[arch] hard for hares, depressing the hare population further. Finally, pred[ator] populations fall due to a shortage of hares for food, allowing the [hare] population to start growing again as its food plants regrow, now e[asier] because few hares are around to browse the plants and stimulate pro[duc]tion of repellant compounds.

Hare population cycles have been studied for nearly a century, lea[ding] to a good understanding of their causes. No one knows, however, [why] the cycle repeats almost exactly every 10 years instead of lasting for [a dif]ferent number of years each time around. At the southern extreme o[f the] snowshoe hare's range, the cycle is dampened and in some places [does] not exist.

Behavior: Snowshoe hares are predominantly nocturnal. During [the] day, they hide under logs, brush and low-hanging conifer branc[hes] crouching still, alert for predators. They forage at night.

Viewing Tips: Drive roads in appropriate habitat at dawn. Easie[r to] find in summer than winter. During spring and autumn, molting [of] hares is sometimes not synchronous with snow melt or snow fall. At t[hese] times, hares can be white when the ground is brown, or brown when [the] ground is white, and relatively easy to see. The hares do not appea[r to] know that they are easy to see and, therefore, remain still and allow v[iew]ers to approach fairly close.

Snowshoe hare molting from its white winter fur to summer's brown pelage.

wshoe hares rely on their white camouflage and staying very still to avoid detection by ators.

April

June

ate change is making time of molt for snowshoe hares to be out of synchrony with early ate snow cover.

e hind feet act as "snowshoes" in the deep powder snow which can blanket the North ds for five to six months of the year.

White-tailed Jackrabbit *Lepus townsendii*

Grassland, prairie, farmland.

Nature Notes:

Some females breed again right after giving birth and, therefore, give birth to a new litter as the offspring in the first litter become independent. The spring and autumn molts are triggered by day length, as they are in snowshoe hares.

Jackrabbit at full speed showing its namesake white tail.

Other Names: prairie hare, jackrabbit

Description: Bigger than a snowshoe h[are]. During summer, yellowish- to grayish-bro[wn] with gray chin and belly; tail entirely white[.] winter, white, ears with black tips. White-ta[iled] jackrabbits can be differentiated from snows[hoe] hares by larger size and appearing lankier a[nd,] in summer, by having a tail that is comple[tely] white; snowshoe hare tails are brown on to[p in] summer.

Size: Weight 5-8 lbs; total length 22-26"; [tail] length 3-4"

Range: From the northern prairies of Can[ada] south into prairies and other open habitats fr[om] the Midwest to the Pacific US states.

Food: Herbivore: in summer, grasses and h[er]baceous vegetation; in winter, inner bark a[nd] buds of shrubs and saplings.

White-tailed jackrabbit on a frosty winter morning. Even its eyelashes are frosty!

Natural History: White-tailed jackrabbits are mammals of open country and are at the eastern-most extent of their range in the North Woods. They start breeding in late winter and can have up to 4 litters, usually of 4 leverets, in summer, depending on food abundance. Newborns weigh about 3 ounces and are fully furred with eyes and ears open. They are independent at roughly one month of age.

Behavior: These hares are predominantly nocturnal, spending most of the day crouching still in a small depression dug next to a bush or rock. They forage singly and spend little time with other hares except for reproduction.

Viewing Tips: White-tailed jackrabbits are easiest to see during spring and autumn molts if their coat color does not match the forest. You are most likely to see these hares at night crossing a road. Their range in the North Woods lies almost completely south of the range of snowshoe hares.

Minn. Rare

Wisc. Rare

Mich.

Eastern Cottontail *Sylvilagus floridanus*

Greatest densities in pasture and grassland where bramble and brush piles predominate but have woodlots interspersed.

Nature Notes:

Females born early in the reproductive season are able to produce kits of their own by late summer, making the extended output of a healthy female even more prodigious.

Foraging peaks at sunrise and sunset.

Foraging on balsam fir needles in winter.

Other Names: cottontail rabbit, bunny

Description: Body red-brown to gray-bro with a somewhat grizzled appearance; usu a red shoulder patch and sometimes a wh forehead patch; tail short, white underneath

Size: Weight 1½ -2½ lbs; total length 16-1 tail length 3-4"

Range: Nearly everywhere in the US east the short grass prairies, except northern N England, eastern Mexico and further south.

Food: Herbivore: in spring and summer, gra es and herbaceous vegetation. In autumn a winter, brambles and inner bark and buds shrubs and saplings. Cottontails raid gard and will girdle and kill healthy saplings in nu eries and suburban yards.

Natural History: Cottontails maintain sm home ranges, often 5 acres or less, and do defend territories. They breed as soon as gr

Cottontails in the North Woods have shorter ears and larger bodies than southern cottontails.

etation appears in spring. Gestation is 30 days and 3-6 leverets are n in a depression lined with fur and covered with vegetation. A moth- pends most of her time away from her young, returning to the nest etively a few times each day to nurse them. When food is abundant, male cottontail can produce up to 7 litters in a year.

havior: During the day, a cottontail often crouches stock still facing from under a bramble patch or brush pile, alert for predators. The ontail slips into thick cover or goes down a hole if a predator comes se. If unable to hide or if surprised, the cottontail makes a sudden zig- dash for safe cover, flashing the white underside of its tail as it runs.

wing Tips: Dawn and k are best times. If you d a nest with young, leave it ne. The mother will return etively and you will prob- y not see her. Do not worry ou touch the youngsters; mother will still return and se them. Will feed beneath d feeders in all seasons.

Beaver   *Castor canadensis*

Wetlands and waterways that have or that can be made to have water deep enough for beavers to swim and, thereby, escape predators.

Nature Notes:

A true ecosystem engineer.

Beavers steer with their tails when swimming, use their tails for stability and support when sitting to cut a tree, and store fat in their tails for winter.

A beaver slaps its tail on the water surface, making a loud "*kerploosh!*" that may warn other colony members of potential danger and that tells predators that the beaver knows they are around.

Other Names: Canadian beaver, No[rth] American beaver

Description: Very large, brown aquatic rod[ent] with relatively small eyes and ears; tail lar[ge] flat, scaled, mostly hairless; hind feet large a[nd] toes webbed.

Size: Weight 35-65 lbs; total length 3-4'; [tail] length 9-12"

Range: In lakes, streams and rivers through[out] North America from northern Canada i[nto] northern Mexico, absent from some of [the] desert Southwest.

Food: Herbivore: in summer, mostly aqua[tic] plants including some aquatic tubers and t[er]restrial leaves and tubers, also inner bark [of] trees; in winter, mostly the inner bark of t[ree] branches in caches. Beavers favor aspens a[nd] birches.

...ary to popular belief, beavers cannot fell a tree in a certain direction. They just chew
...hew until it falls. Fortunately, most trees have more crown mass on the sunny side which
...en over the water.

...ural History: Beavers live in colonies, which are extended fam-
...roups including a pair of parents and offspring from recent years.
...a colony maintains a territory that is not shared with other beavers.
...itories are scent marked using castor mounds, which are piles of mud
...vegetation topped with a deposit from the beavers' castor glands.
...se paired glands are found on either side of a beaver's anus close to
...beavers' anal glands, which secrete different compounds.

...rritory may include the shore of part of a lake or river, or a length of
...m, or several ponds. Where waterways are too shallow for beavers
...wim, beavers build dams, often series of dams, providing access,

...swimming, to a length of
...m that provides sufficient
...l. Ponds created by dams
...ide access to trees for win-
...ood and to aquatic vegeta-
... As beavers remove trees
...winter food, they extend
...r system of dams to gain
...ss to new trees. Materials

Lodges are the homes for beaver families. Not to be confused with dams, which are stric water control structures.

for a dam include mud, rocks, sticks and logs.

Within its territory, each colony has a lodge or bank den. A bank de a hole in a river bank or steep lake shore having an underwater entr but a living space above water level. A lodge is a pile of sticks, mud rocks in a lake or pond, again having under-water entrances only above water living spaces.

Beavers are highly adapted to chew down trees to reach the inner b or cambium, of branches. They use their large incisor teeth, powe by huge jaw muscles, to chew and leverage chips of wood from a trunk, eventually felling the tree. Although beavers eat cambium du summer, small branches provide food for beavers all winter. Beaver a colony build a cache of branches in the water near their lodge or c In winter, most of the cache is underwater, so beavers can reach it ur the ice, cut a branch, and take the branch back to the lodge or den to

The tops of beavers' cheek teeth are criss-crossed with complex loops topped with enamel, which allow them to shred tough plant materials. For most of each beaver's life, the cheek teeth

Beaver hauling a branch, either back to its lodge to store underwater for winter food, or to use in construction of its lodge or dam.

e open roots and continue to grow, just matching the speed at which
teeth are worn down.

r humans, wolves are the most important predators of beavers, mostly
n lakes are not frozen. Occasionally coyotes, bobcats, black bears,
rs or a passing puma prey on beavers. For all predators, a beaver
es a formidable foe with its large incisors and strong jaws. Most

ers are killed on land,
re they fell trees and
re they are least agile.

vers breed during
ter in their lodges.
r a 15 week gesta-
, kits (usually 3-4) are
i in late spring or
y summer. A kit stays
s natal colony for 2-3
s and then disperses
ind either a place to
blish a new colony or
ind a colony that has
an adult to wolves or
trapper. Where they
not trapped, many
ers live to be 10-15
s old.

A beaver carries mud and debris to patch its dam. Beavers
do not carry mud on their tails.

avior: Beavers are
tly nocturnal dur-
the ice-free period.
ally one or more col-
members are active
our or so before dark
swim around the
ny's territory. They often inspect dams and forage on aquatic vegeta-
. Sometimes they come on shore to work at cutting down a tree. All
nbers of a colony will bring branches from a fallen tree to the colony's
ter cache.

wing Tips: The best time to see beavers is evening when boating
waterway that has an obvious lodge or dam. Be quiet and enjoy the
v.

Porcupine *Erethizon dorsatum*

Places with trees. Although porcupines forage in grasslands and forest openings, they depend on trees in winter.

Nature Notes:

Porcupine tracks are easy to identify in winter because porcupines walk with the toes on their forefeet facing in (photo below).

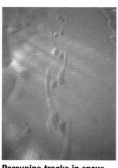

Porcupine tracks in snow; note the inward pointing toes and the tail drag marks.

Other Names: quill pig, hedgehog, porc-e North American porcupine, porky

Description: Unmistakable, large rod mostly covered by quills. Body gray to bro gray to black with long silver guard hairs top of head, shoulders, legs and belly; mu and nose black, without quills; paws black long claws; ears small; eyes black; center of b has rosette of prominent quills with few gu hairs; belly has few to no quills.

Size: 12-30 lbs; total length 2-3'; tail length

Range: From tundra in Alaska and Car south along the western Mountains, south the North Woods, east to New York and N England in the US.

Food: Herbivore: in spring, catkins of wi and poplar; in summer, grasses, herbaceous etation; in autumn, fruit, nuts; in winter, ir bark of diverse trees.

...s how we often see porcupines—high up in a tree, feasting on the inner bark of branches.

...ural History: Home ranges may be 50 acres or more in summer ...only 5 acres or smaller in winter if a porcupine finds a winter den ...winter food trees nearby. Winter dens are usually hollow trees, hol-...logs or small caves, under buildings or in the corner of a collapsed ...ding.

...predators kill porcupines. Pumas kill porcupines occasionally but ...ers are truly specialists at killing porcupines. Where their ranges over-...fishers sometimes limit porcupine populations. To be able to kill a ...cupine, a fisher must find it on the ground without a place for the ...cupine to hide its face.

...cupines breed in the late ...or early winter and females ...birth in spring to a sin-...large, precocial youngster, ...etimes called a porcupette. ...nates are fully furred, with ...ls, have their eyes and ears ...n, and can eat soft foods. ...they do nurse and stay

Minn.

Wisc.

Mich.

In spring, porcupines seek out the newly-emerged catkins of willows and poplars.

with their mothers until autumn. Porcupines communicate with m
soft sounds and with a nasal "*onk.*"

Porcupines chew sweat-impregnated handles of tools and treated lum
to get salt. The tops of porcupines' cheek teeth are criss-crossed v
complex loops topped with enamel, which allow them to shred to
plant materials.

Behavior: Porcupines are largely nocturnal. In summer, they tend
rest in trees. In winter, porcupines rest in their dens with their backs
tails facing out all day, then walk to their nearby food trees in ever
and back before dawn. In their food trees, porcupines clip the pencil-t
ends of branches and let them fall, then select the next size of branche
debark, eating the inner bark. Deer often eat the small conifer branc
and needles that porcupines drop. Porcupines in trees usually face a
from tree trunks, protecting them from fishers that climb the trees.

When threatened on the ground, porcupines protect their faces by fit

n into niches among rocks, between roots at tree trunks and against
. When a predator approaches, a porcupine humps its back and flips
il up, driving quills into the predator.

wing Tips: Look for round dark "blobs" in winter trees; if it isn't a
rrel nest, it could be a porky! Porcupines are often seen at night along
ls, where they eat grasses and herbaceous vegetation. Because they do
flee from predators, they are frequent road kills

up when you see porcupine droppings on the ground; there may be a porky working in
ee above.

porcupines are as cute as their name, "porcupettes." Light patches on these aspens are
esult of heavy feeding by a porcupine.

White-footed Mouse *Peromyscus leucopus*

Grasslands, farmland, forests. Often in houses/outbuildings in winter.

Nature Notes:

White-footed mice sometimes enter torpor during winter.

Other Names: wood mouse, deer mouse

Description: A pretty mouse; body go[ ]brown to brown; underside bright white; and ears large; tail usually indistinctly bi[ ]ored, with short, brown fur on top, w[ ]fur underneath, and a blurred line where[ ]contrasting colors meet. Juveniles' fur [ ]on sides and back; not brown like ad[ ]Not always possible to differentiate from [ ]mouse, which usually has a sharp line on[ ]between contrasting colors. Where their ra[ ]overlap in the North Woods, white-footed r[ ]are somewhat more likely than deer mice t[ ]in open habitats.

Size: Weight ½-1 oz.; total length 6-8"; length 3-5"

Range: From the Great Plains eastw[ ]excluding Canada and Florida, extending [ ]eastern Mexico.

od: Omnivore: seeds, nuts, berries, fruit, green vegetation, insects.

ural History: Territories of white-footed mice can be less than
acre. During breeding season, females maintain territories that
lap with those of males.

mammalian and avian predators are happy to eat white-footed
e. Hawks and owls eat many, as do coyotes, bobcats, red foxes,
foxes and especially weasels. Weasels follow them down holes,
ugh subnivean spaces in winter, and up shrubs and trees. Few
te-footed mice live longer than a year.

h mortality from predation is offset by high reproductive rates.
ales begin breeding as vegetation turns green in spring and some-
es produce 4 litters or more in summer and early autumn. Litter
is usually 4-6. Incisors erupt at 4-5 days, ears open at 10 days, and
at 12 days. Young are on their own by 4 weeks of age. Young
te-footed mice molt to their adult brown coats when they start
ding, at 6-7 weeks of age.

avior: White-footed mice are active from dusk to dawn, occa-
ally during the day. They hoard seeds for winter. They are good
bers and harvest fruit and nuts from shrubs and trees.

wing Tips: People are most likely to see white-footed mice in
r houses or garages in winter. They often explore campsites of
rs and canoeists, chewing into food bags and stealing nuts and
d fruit for their caches. At night outside a tent, they sound much
er than they are.

Minn.

Wisc.

Mich.

Deer Mouse   *Peromyscus maniculatus*

Most forest habitats. Often found in houses/outbuildings in winter.

Nature Notes:

Populations in houses can be quite high in winter. We trapped over two dozen deer mice in the cabinet under our bathroom sink one winter. The short-tailed weasel who snuck into the basement of another house kept the deer mouse population in check there all winter.

Other Names: wood mouse, woodl mouse, woodland deer mouse

Description: A very pretty mouse; body g en brown to brown; underside bright wh eyes and ears large; tail usually bicolored short, brown fur on top, white fur underne and a distinct line where the contrasting co meet. Juvenile fur gray on sides and back; brown like adults. Not always possible to di entiate from white-footed mouse, which usu has a blurred line on tail between contras colors. Where their ranges overlap in the N Woods, deer mice are somewhat more li than white-footed mice to be in forest habi

Size: Weight ½-1 oz.; total length 6-8"; length 3-5"

Range: Found throughout most of N America from the northern boreal forests Mexico but absent in southeast US beyond Appalachian Mountains.

od: Omnivore: seeds, nuts, berries, fruit, green vegetation, insects.

tural History: Home ranges of deer mice are usually a few acres. ales may maintain territories during the breeding season, otherwise e ranges of deer mice overlap. In winter, groups of a dozen or more share a tree cavity, a hole in the ground under the snow, or a bird . They are active under the snow but also ascend to the snow surface, n along a sloping branch, to forage for seeds.

mammalian and avian predators are happy to eat deer mice. Hawks owls eat many, as do coyotes, bobcats, gray foxes, red foxes and espe-ly weasels. Weasels can follow them down holes, through subnivean es in winter, and up shrubs and trees. Few deer mice live longer than ar.

h mortality from predation is offset by high reproductive rates. ales begin breeding as vegetation turns green in spring and some-es produce as many as 4 litters or more in summer and early autumn. er size is usually 3-5 and young are on their own by 4 weeks of age. ng deer mice molt to their adult brown coats when they start breed-at 5-7 weeks of age.

havior: Deer mice are active from dusk to dawn but rarely during the . They hoard seeds for winter. We found a hoard in our wood box summer that was as big as a softball, filled mostly with wild buck-at and grass seeds. By early winter, hoards are larger. Deer mice are d climbers and harvest from shrubs and trees.

wing Tips: People are most likely to see deer mice in their houses or ges in winter. They often explore campsites of hikers and canoeists, wing into food bags and stealing nuts and dried fruit for their caches. night outside a tent, they sound much bigger than they are.

Southern Red-backed Vole   *Myodes gapperi*

Forests; favoring those with logs and low conifer branches.

Nature Notes:

We enjoy watching the red-backed voles under our bird feeders in winter as much as watching the birds. We often see voles foraging on the forest floor, zipping between logs on the ground and tunnels into the snow.

Red-backed voles have several foraging periods a day, separated by rest. They are active all winter, mostly under the snow.

Other Names: red-backed mouse, red-bac vole. Formerly known as *Clethrionomys gapp*

Description: Medium-sized to small cute v rusty band running from head to rump; and eyes small; tail short.

Size: Weight ¾-1½ oz.; total length 5-7"; length 1-2"

Range: Throughout the boreal forests North America extending south along Rocky Mountains, the Appalachian Mounta and south of Lake Superior.

Food: Herbivore: in summer, grasses, her ceous vegetation, seeds, nuts, berries, fru fungi and lichens, some insects; in win seeds, inner bark of roots and saplings.

Natural History: All mammalian and av predators eat red-backed voles, especially w sels. Breed as soon as green vegetation app

ave to be a sharp-eyed naturalist to find a nest of red-backed voles. Four to five is the aver-
tter size, and the female can produce several litters in a season.

allen seeds below a North Woods feeding station are a boon for hungry red-backed voles.

pring, producing several litters of 4-5 young in a year. Young reach
al maturity by 3 months. Populations fluctuate from hundreds per
 to nearly none.

Minn.

Wisc.

Mich.

Eastern Heather Vole   *Phenacomys ungava*

Open coniferous forest with shrubby understory or near wet meadows.

Nature Notes:

Elusive North Woods resident.

Heather voles forage in the evening and at night, often caching food near a tunnel to eat during the day.

Build underground nests with tunnels leading to several entrances.

Other Names: Ungava vole

Description: Medium sized vole; body g zled brown with a yellowish wash; tail sh eyes small; ears barely visible above fur.

Size: Weight 1-1½ oz.; total length 5-6"; ta length 1-1½"

Range: Southern range limit at Canad north shores of Lakes Superior and Hu north through Canada's boreal forests.

Food: Herbivore: leaves, berries, seeds, lich fungus, inner bark of shrubs.

Natural History: Secretive. Mart weasels and other predators eat th when they can catch th Reproductive season l from May through Aug Females produce litters 2-8 pups after a 30 day tation. Pups can reprod when 1½ months old.

Minn.

Wisc.

Mich.

ck (Yellownosed) Vole *Microtus chrotorrhinus*

ssy rocks in pristine northern mixed forests.

Nature Notes:

A vole of rocky habitats.

Rock voles cut herbaceous vegetation that they pull into their tiny caves amongst the rocks.

er Names: yellow-nosed vole

scription: Medium-sized vole; back brown; zle with distinct yellow to orange wash; and ears small. Differs from other voles by ng the yellow wash on its muzzle.

e: Weight 1-1¾ oz.; total length 6"; tail th 1½-2"

ge: West from southeast Labrador to h of Lake Superior, and southwest to the al forests of the southern Appalachians.

d: Herbivore: herbaceous vegetation, chberry.

ural History: The breed-
season begins in early
ch and lasts until late
mn. Litter size is 3-4.
ales breed right after
ng birth and deliver the
litter when the first litter
omes independent.

Minn.

Wisc.

Mich.

Meadow Vole *Microtus pennsylvanicus*

Grasslands, pastures, meadows.

Nature Notes:

The most prolific wild mammal on earth.

Meadow voles have several foraging periods a day, separated by rest. They build thatched above-ground tunnels through their territories that connect to above-ground nests and underground tunnels.

Other Names: meadow mouse, field mou

Description: Large brown to gray-brown v belly gray, eyes and ears small. Distinguis from rock vole by not having yellow on muz larger than pine vole, having larger eyes ears, longer tail, color not uniform brown.

Size: Weight 1-2¼ oz.; total length 6-7"; length 1-2"

Range: From tundra south through bo forests, down the Rocky Mountains, into northern Great Plains, and into the east deciduous forest but not to the deep so of the US.

Food: Herbivore: grasses, baceous vegetation and se occasionally insects.

Natural History: Fem maintain territories t may be a quarter of an a All mammalian and av

Minn.

Wisc.

Mich.

lators eat meadow voles and their population fluctuations drive the ulation sizes of many predators. The breeding season begins in early ng and lasts until late autumn, with winter breeding when food is ndant. A female meadow vole breeds within a day after giving birth litter of 3-10 pups, delivering her next litter in about 3 weeks, when s in the present litter become independent.

male who has 8 litters in a year and whose young and their young n reproducing when two months old will be responsible for about new voles that year. Thus, meadow vole populations irrupt, overeat r food supplies, and then crash over 2-4 year periods.

s are the "bread and butter" of many northern predators. The Rough-legged Hawk (top eating intestines of vole), survives and thrives on voles, as do Northern Hawk Owls (top ‚ Northern Harriers (bottom right) and coyotes.

Pine (Woodland) Vole *Microtus pinetorum*

Forested areas with shrubs; also nurseries, orchards and suburban lots.

Nature Notes:

Pine voles sometimes girdle ornamental shrubs and fruit trees.

Pine voles live in extended family groups that maintain territories with systems of thatch-covered trenches. All members of an extended family group maintain the trench system, bring seeds and nuts to a cache, and huddle with newborns.

Other Names: woodland vole, mole mou...

Description: Small vole; back dark chest... brown; eyes and ears very small; tail short.

Size: Weight ½-1¼ oz.; total length 4-5"; length ½-1"

Range: Restricted to eastern forests of the... excluding Florida.

Food: Herbivore: seeds, nuts year round, c... bium of roots and shrubs in winter.

Natural History: A family group has a pai... adults and young from recent litters. Litter... is usually two.

Minn.

Wisc.

Mich.

outhern Bog Lemming *Synaptomys cooperi*

...verse forests and grasslands.

...er Names: southern lemming mouse

...scription: Small vole; body uniform brown; ...d slightly large with hairs that exaggerate its ...; eyes and ears small; upper incisors have ...gitudinal grooves.

...e: Weight ¾-1¾ oz.; total length 4-6"; tail ...gth ½-1"

...ge: From the North Woods south to cen- ...US, east to St Lawrence Seaway, south to ...ral Atlantic states.

...d: Herbivore: grasses, her- ...ous vegetation.

...ural History: They can ...d year round, presumably ...n winter food is abun- ...t. Gestation is about 3½ ...ks and young reach adult ...in 3 weeks.

Nature Notes:

Despite their name, these rodents are not restricted to living in bogs and have tails long enough for them to be considered voles.

Most active during dawn and dusk with several active periods each day.

Not well known because their population densities are usually low.

Muskrat   *Ondatra zibethicus*

Marshes and diverse wetlands, usually near shallow water with emerge͏ vegetation.

Nature Notes:

The world's largest vole.

A foraging muskrat can remain submerged for as long as 15 minutes. It uses its tail as a rudder when swimming.

Other Names: mudcat, musquash, m͏ beaver

Description: A huge, semi-aquatic vole; ͏ form brown with paler belly; long, coarse g͏ hairs cover thick, soft underfur; tail long, m͏ ly hairless, flattened laterally; hind feet web͏

Size: Weight 1½-4 lbs; total length 1½-2'; length 7-12"

Range: From tundra in Canada and Alask͏ southern US, absent in hot and dry habitat͏

Food: Herbivore mostly: aquatic vegetat͏ especially cattails and rushes; occasionally c͏ fish, mussels, small fish.

Natural History: Muskrats build hou͏ or lodges, of cut cattails and other vegeta͏ in marshes. A lodge is above water level͏ dry within, having a few tunnels that lea͏ underwater entrances. Muskrats also dig ͏

...guished from beaver by its smaller size and by swimming with back above the water ...ail trailing in an S-curve, while beaver swims with only head showing. Muskrat house ...orth Woods marsh.

...with underwater entrances leading to a dry room above water level. ...ks, otters, raccoons and coyotes are the most important predators. ...e North Woods, muskrats produce up to 3 litters of 6-7 kits in a ...oductive season that lasts all summer. Youngsters can swim by 2 ...s of age and are weaned by 4 weeks. Young might stay with their ...er through winter but are independent by spring, when they start ...ducing. In the northern parts of the muskrat's range, populations ...in synchrony with snowshoe hare populations.

...**avior:** Muskrats forage
...ly during darkness but
...ctive occasionally during
...ay.

...**ving Tips:** Look for
...rat scats (which look like
...mouse droppings) on
...near emergent vegetation
...eams, ponds and lakes.

Woodland Jumping Mouse *Napeozapus insign*

Seldom found outside forest cover.

Nature Notes:

Can not be confused with any other mouse because of very long tail with white tip and very large hind feet

Woodland jumping mice are nocturnal. They do not make runways but use those built by other rodents.

Hibernate in winter.

Description: Small mouse with long h feet and very long tail tipped with white h back brown, sides are yellow to golden us with an orange wash; upper incisors have a tinct longitudinal groove; more colorful t meadow jumping mouse.

Size: Weight ¾ -1 oz.; total length 8-10"; length 5-6"

Range: From the North Woods east to Labr and south to the southern Appalachians.

Food: Herbivore to omnivore: fungi can third of the diet, also caterpillars, beetles seeds of jewelweed.

Natural History: Litters of young are born in late Jun early July after gestation o about 29 days. Young becc independent at about on month of age, less than week after opening their e

Minn.

Wisc.

Mich.

eadow Jumping Mouse *Zapus hudsonius*

st common in grasslands but will live in forests.

cription: Small mouse with long hind
and very long tail not tipped with white;
brown, sides are yellow to golden; upper
sors have a distinct longitudinal groove; less
rful than woodland jumping mouse.

e: Weight ½-1 oz.; total length 7-10"; tail
th 4-6"

ge: Across the boreal forests of Canada
h into the Great Plains and east to the
ntic coast but not the deep South.

d: Herbivore to omnivore: fungi, jewel-
d, invertebrates, seeds and fruit.

ural History: Up to 3
rs of 3-6 young are born
ear after gestation of about
ays. Young born in late
mer may not gain enough
o survive hibernation.

Nature Notes:

Meadow jumping mice are
nocturnal.

Rats *Rattus* species

Mostly in urban areas, farms and grain elevators.

Nature Notes:

Several species of the genus *Rattus* have been transported around the world, especially via international shipping. Extensive hybridization often prevents identification of rats to species.

Rats are most active at night to avoid their human benefactors.

Other Names: "The" rat, brown rat, ship black rat, Norway rat, warf rat, sewer rat

Description: Color varied from brown to to black; belly gray; eyes and ears not large mostly hairless, with dark scales; tail ca longer or shorter than the body.

Size: Weight 5-10 oz.; body 6-8 inches; length 12-18"

Range: Throughout North America but ly absent in extensive forest.

Food: Omnivore: foods available from pe in and around buildings, on farms an grain elevators, supplemented with seeds, insects including roaches and wild foods.

Natural History: Females can produce se litters of 4-10 pups each year. Pups indepen by 3 weeks of age. Rats have complex s groups with complicated mating behavior.

...use **Mouse** *Mus musculus*

...an areas, on farms and at grain elevators. Wild populations in urban ...as live along highways and in parks and cemeteries.

...cription: Body usually gray, sometimes ...vn, even a pretty golden brown; belly gray; ... and ears not as large as those of deer mice; ... long, mostly hairless, with gray scales. To ...nguish from deer mice and white-footed ...e, look first at the tail.

...e: Weight ½-1 oz.; total length 6-7"; tail ...th 2½-3½"

...ge: Throughout North America but most-...)sent in extensive forest.

...d: Omnivore: wild house mice eat grasses, ...aceous vegetation, leaves of shrubs, seeds, ..., berries, fruit and insects; in winter, inner ... of shrubs and saplings.

...ural History: Females can produce several ...rs of 4-8 pups each year. Pups are born hair-...with eyes and ears closed but are indepen-...: by 2 weeks of age.

Nature Notes:

Whether just 1 or 2 or more species of the genus *Mus* have become commensal and whether they hybridize is uncertain.

House mice are most active at night to avoid their human benefactors.

Individuals from wild populations move in and out of buildings, often related to weather.

Least Chipmunk *Tamias minimus*

Mostly mixed forests with a significant conifer component.

Nature Notes:

Our smallest squirrel.

Home ranges can be as large as 15 acres.

Least chipmunks have fur-lined cheek pouches for carrying seeds.

They are prey for hawks, weasels, foxes, bobcats and other predators.

Least chipmunks hibernate in winter.

Note the closely spaced back stripes, which helps distinguish this species from the eastern chipmunk.

Other Names: Formerly *Eutamias minimu* then *Neotamias minimus*.

Description: Smaller than eastern chipmu Brown and white stripes from nose to ru otherwise brown to gray-brown with rusty si tail brown mixed with gray. Distinguished f eastern chipmunk by smaller size, stripes face more obvious, lack of rusty patches rump, back stripes closely spaced.

Size: Weight 1¼-2 oz.; total length 8-9"; length 3-4"

Range: Boreal forests from the Great Lake the Yukon, south into western Great Plains west into mountain ranges.

Food: Herbivore: seeds, also flowers, b leaves, insects.

Natural History: Least chipmunks b shortly after coming out of hibernation

...st chipmunks show well-defined face stripes and very closely-spaced back stripes. These ...features help separate this species from its cousin the eastern chipmunk in areas where ...r ranges overlap.

...30 days later produce a litter of 3-8 naked, blind young, born in a ...e in the ground. Youngsters appear above ground when 3 weeks old, ...only some 30% of them will survive to breed the following spring. ...ult female least chipmunks occasionally produce a second litter in late ...mmer.

...havior: Least chipmunks are diurnal, foraging for grass seeds much of ...day and storing them in a central cache. The area around the cache ...efended against other chipmunks. Least chipmunks spend nights and ...winter in a set of tunnels under ground or in rocks or logs.

...ewing Tips: The stripes ...chipmunks might seem ...vious but they can make ...pmunks surprisingly ...ptic, especially where the ...und has spots of sunlight ...d shadows. Often seen ...r backyard bird feeders, ...mpsites.

Eastern Chipmunk   *Tamius striatus*

Mostly mixed forests with a significant conifer component.

Nature Notes:

Chipmunk with a rusty rump.

Eastern chipmunks have fur-lined cheek pouches for carrying seeds.

Widely spaced back stripes help separate the eastern chipmunk from the least, which has closely spaced stripes.

Description: Larger than least chipmu[nk]. Back has two black stripes with white str[ipe] between on each side, otherwise brown to gr[ay] brown with rusty rump; belly pale; tail bro[wn] mixed with gray. Distinguished from le[ast] chipmunk by larger size, stripes on face [less] obvious, widely spaced back stripes and ru[sty] patches on rump.

Size: Weight 3-5 oz.; total length 9-10"; [tail] length 3-4"

Range: Throughout eastern North Amer[ica] from southern boreal forests into the de[ep] South.

Food: Herbivore: seeds, nuts, flowers, bu[ds,] leaves, insects.

Natural History: Eastern chipmunks are p[rey] for hawks, weasels, red foxes, bobcats and ot[her] predators.

Eastern chipmunks hibernate in winter. Th[ey] breed shortly after coming out of hibernati[on]

...the lack of distinct dark facial stripes compared to those of the least chipmunk.

...produce a litter of 4-5 naked, blind young a month later in a hole ...he ground. Youngsters nurse for 6 weeks. When food is abundant, ...g might breed in late summer, when their mothers might produce ...cond litter.

...avior: Eastern chipmunks are diurnal, foraging for grass seeds and ...ng them in a central cache, mostly during a morning and an after-...n foraging period. Eastern chipmunks spend nights and all winter in ...of tunnels under ground or in rocks or logs.

...wing Tips: The stripes of chipmunks might seem obvious but they ...make chipmunks surprisingly cryptic, especially where the ground ...spots of sunlight and shadows. Often seen near backyard bird feed-...campsites.

...k pouches allow a chipmunk to
...many seeds back to its cache.

Minn.

Wisc.

Mich.

Family *Sciuridae* SQUIRRELS | **153**

Woodchuck *Marmota monax*

Habitat edges between brushy forest and open areas, such as fields, roads and power line rights-of-way.

Nature Notes:

The flatland marmot.

Mother Woodchucks use a sharp whistle to warn offspring of danger.

Looking like a stump but alert to danger on its hind legs, a woodchuck may give a loud sharp call to warn young of possible trouble.

Other Names: groundhog, whistle pig

Description: Large ground squirrel; thic body grizzled brown to gray; belly redd brown; ears rounded and short; tail short bushy; feet with 4 toes and sturdy claws.

Size: Weight 6-10 lbs; total length 1½-2'; length 4-6"

Range: Most of Canada's boreal forest. In US from the eastern prairies to the Atla coast and into the deep South.

Food: Herbivore: grasses, herbaceous veg tion, seeds; in summer, sometimes gar vegetables; in spring, inner bark and bud shrubs and trees.

Natural History: Woodchucks have territe of up to 10 acres with little to no overlap. T dig holes and tunnels for natal dens to young, for rest sites, for hibernation sites

ring, woodchucks have litters of two to seven "chucklings" (yes, that is a term). The
g can also be called kits or cubs.

escape from predators, such as coyotes, bobcats and badgers. They
etimes dig holes under houses.

odchucks mate after emerging from hibernation and produce a single
ual litter of 2-7 naked young about a month later. Young are weaned
bout 1½ months of age and fend for themselves thereafter.

havior: Woodchucks are solitary except to mate and for mothers and
r young. They are diurnal but generally have morning and afternoon
vity peaks. During summer, they gain large amounts of fat to support
m through hibernation.

wing Tips: Woodchucks
dom travel far from escape
es. While they forage, they
en sit up on their hind legs
chew a plant while smell-
, listening and looking
predators. Listen for the
istle and look for a short
st" in a field (see photo in
ebar on opposite page).

Franklin's Ground Squirrel *Poliocitellus frankli*

In the North Woods, prefer edges between forest and open land, forest fragmentation caused by people. Distribution very patchy.

Nature Notes:

Relatively new resident to the North Woods.

Winter mortality is as high as 50 percent, probably due to both starvation and predation.

Named in 1822 for British Arctic explorer Sir John Franklin by Joseph Sabine, who first described this species.

Other Names: gray ground squirrel, g gopher, bush gopher, formerly *Spermophilus*

Description: Body yellow-brown, mott with black; head gray with white eye ring; small and round; tail mixed gray and white.

Size: Weight 1-1¼ lbs; total length 14-16"; length 5-6"

Range: Eastern Great Plains and prairie la of Canada into Alberta.

ange of Franklin's ground squirrels has been moving north slowly.

d: Herbivore to omnivore: herbaceous vegetation, seeds, but some-
es toads, small mammals, birds and eggs.

tural History: Home ranges can be as large as 60 acres for males
20 acres for females, with considerable overlap. Predators include
cats, coyotes, badgers and hawks.

nklin's ground squirrels mate after emerging from hibernation and
ales produce a single, annual litter of usually 7-9 young 3½-4 weeks
r. Youngsters are weaned when a month old and are adult size by the
e they enter hibernation in early autumn.

havior: Franklin's ground squirrels are perhaps the least social of
und squirrels. Although home ranges overlap, the squirrels mostly
id each other.

wing Tips: Adults
er hibernation as early
ate July, so from August
October most of the
nklin's ground squirrels
and about are juveniles.

Thirteen-lined Ground Squirrel
Ictidomys tridecemlineatus

Native of short-grass prairie but now adapted to humans' lawns, golf courses, cemeteries and roadsides.

Nature Notes:

Thirteen-lined ground squirrels double their weight in late summer to survive hibernation.

Minnesota is nicknamed the "Gopher State," but the name is a misnomer as the "gopher" is actually the thirteen-lined ground squirrel. The "Ground Squirrel State" doesn't have the same ring.

Other Names: striped gopher, thirteen-li gopher, striped ground squirrel, thirteen li tridec. Formerly *Spermophilus tridecemlineat*

Description: Slender body; back covered w alternating light brown and dark brown stri with light spots in the dark stripes; tail mi dark and light hairs.

Size: Weight 4-9 oz.; total length 8-11"; length 3-5"

Range: The Great Plains from Canada do to Texas, extending east through the Midwe

Food: Herbivore to Omnivore: grass se herbaceous vegetation, caterpillars, grassh pers, beetles, beetle larvae.

Natural History: Thirteen-lined ground squirrels dig tunnels for raising young, resti and escaping from predators, which include Red-tailed Hawks, Swainson's Hawks, badg

pen area will do...even a beach on Lake Superior's shore. Note the numerous back stripes.

tes and bobcats. These rrels mate upon emerg- from hibernation and 6-13 ng are born 4 weeks later. ng are independent at 6 ks and reach adult weight e 5 weeks later.

avior: Thirteen-lined nd squirrels are diurnal are active much of the day. y usually stay close to holes may be short escape tun- or that may be connected ong tunnels. The squirrels n sit up near a hole, ready ive if alarmed. They give a ng alarm call to warn off- ng of danger.

wing Tips: Watch for teen-lined ground squir- sitting up along roadsides n large lawns at cemeteries golf courses.

You may have to use your imagination, but there really are 13 stripes on their backs; stripes are also excellent camouflage for a grassland species.

Minn.

Wisc.

Mich.

Gray Squirrel *Sciurus carolinensis*

Gray squirrels are forest mammals that have adapted to urban habitats as well. Most common in broad-leaved forests.

Nature Notes:

Gray squirrels remember all scatter-hoarded nuts and sometimes move nuts if they believe that hiding places were seen by other squirrels.

Home ranges are usually less than 5 acres in forests with significant numbers of broad-leaved trees that produce large nuts.

Albino gray squirrels will always have pink eyes.

Other Names: eastern gray squirrel

Description: Body gray, sometimes wit red to orange wash, but black and white c phases can be locally common; tail gray m with brown, black and white. Distinguis from fox squirrel by smaller size, gray belly smaller amount of orange highlights in fur.

Size: Weight ¾ -1¾ lbs; total length 1¼-1 tail length 6-10"

Range: Throughout eastern US into south Ontario, Quebec and NW into southern Albe

Food: Herbivore to omnivore: nuts, se flowers and buds, mushrooms, large inse birds and eggs, in winter inner bark of branc

Natural History: Home ranges usually o lap with those of several other gray squir Diverse mammalian and avian predators ca significant population decreases of squir through winter.

...y squirrels are very arboreal, and quite at home climbing and leaping from tree to tree. ...e are areas where black phase gray squirrels are quite common (left) and also populations ...ucistic gray squirrels (right). These white squirrels have dark eyes and so are NOT albinos.

...y squirrels start breeding as early as mid-winter, producing litters in ...e cavities some 6 weeks later. Litter size is commonly 2-3 and new-...ns are naked and blind. By 8-9 weeks of age, young are independent. ...nale gray squirrels often have a second litter in summer.

...havior: Gray squirrels are diurnal. They harvest nuts from trees or ...s that fall to the ground and bury them to eat later. Gray squirrels ...vive winter eating their scatter-hoarded nuts.

...wing Tips: Gray squirrels are common in towns throughout the ...rth Woods, except in the far north. Wherever you see them in towns, ... will also find them in the surrounding forests. Common at feeders.

Eastern Fox Squirrel   *Sciurus niger*

Prefer more open forests than do gray squirrels.

Nature Notes:

Fox squirrels remember all scatter-hoarded nuts and sometimes move nuts if they believe that hiding places were seen by other squirrels.

Diurnal squirrel.

Description: Body gray, with an orange w but black color phase can be locally comm belly orange; tail orange mixed with bla Other, very diverse color phases live in southeast United States. Distinguished fr gray squirrel by larger size, orange belly abundance of orange highlights in fur.

Size: Weight 1¼-3 lbs; total length 1½-2¼'; length 8-12"

Range: Throughout most of eastern US exc the northern Great Lakes and New England Great Plains, range follows riverine forests.

Food: Herbivore to omnivore: nuts, se flowers, buds, mushrooms, large insects, b and eggs; in winter; inner bark of branches.

Natural History: Home ranges of fox squir can reach 50 acres and their densities never as high as do gray squirrel populations. Div mammalian and avian predators cause sigr

nuts are a large part of the fox squirrel's diet.

population decreases of squirrels through winter.

squirrels start breeding as early as mid-winter, producing litters in cavities or leaf nests some 6 weeks later. Litter size is commonly 2-3 newborns are naked and blind. By 12 weeks of age, they are indepen- t. Female fox squirrels often have a second litter in summer. Young not reach adult size until a year old.

havior: Fox squirrels harvest nuts from trees or nuts that fall to the und and bury them for later. Fox squirrels are more likely than gray irrels to forage on the ground and to travel on the ground instead hrough treetops. They also tend to venture further from trees when ging than do gray squirrels. Fox squirrels survive winter eating their ter-hoarded nuts.

wing Tips: Fox squirrels common in towns with- their range in the North ods. Wherever you see n in towns, you will find n in the surrounding open sts. Uncommon in woods y from towns in our region.

Red Squirrel *Tamiasciurus hudsonicus*

Forests with a significant conifer component.

Nature Notes:

Good middens may be used by a succession of red squirrels.

Move with great dexterity in trees, making them difficult to catch. Martens are also skilled climbers yet catch most in squirrels' middens in winter.

Other Names: chickaree, pine squirrel, b[...]ing pine squirrel, boomer

Description: Body rusty-red in summer, g[...] red in winter; belly white with black line se[...] rating body and belly color; eye has white ri[...] tail mixed red, black and yellow.

Size: Weight 8-10 oz.; total length 1-1¼'; [...] length 4-6"

Range: From northern boreal forests ac[...] Alaska and Canada south down the Ro[...] Mountains and south to Indiana in the Midv[...] and southern Appalachian Mountains.

Food: Herbivore to omnivore: conifer se[...] and some deciduous seeds, mushrooms, la[...] insects, small vertebrates, birds and eggs.

Natural History: Red squirrels maintain [...] ritories that are announced many times a [...] with a loud *chr-r-r-r-r-r-r-r-r* call that [...] other red squirrels that the territory is occup[...] Neighboring squirrels respect each other's [...]

squirrels eat and cache mushrooms (top left). A well-used midden (top right). Feasting
tamarack buds (middle right). Amazing leapers. Will use natural cavities for roosting.

ries and recognize each neighbor's calls. Red squirrels harvest cones
n conifers and store them in one or more caches, or "middens." A
lden is often under a root mass or in a hole within a hollow tree and
contents often spills out onto the forest floor.

rt breeding in late winter but females usually have only one litter per
r. Courtship is noisy with much chasing and vocalizing. Gestation
s about 5 weeks and young are born naked in tree cavities with eyes
ears closed. Young are weaned and independent some 6 weeks later.

havior: Diurnal and can be active any time during the day, summer
winter. When seeds begin to ripen in cones, squirrels will climb
ough trees, cutting cones and letting them drop. The squirrels then
ner them and cache them
their middens. Red squir-
often harvest mushrooms
lay them out to dry on
nches.

wing Tips: Listen for the
d *chr-r-r-r-r-r-r-r-r-r* terri-
al call. Often invite them-
es to bird feeding stations.

Flying Squirrels *Glaucomys sabrinus & G. volans*

Northern flying squirrels found mostly in areas with some conifer trees in the forest, southern flying squirrels not so much so.

Nature Notes:

Flying squirrels sometimes make leaf nests in chimneys, blocking the draft and causing fireworks out the chimney top if the nest catches fire.

Home ranges vary from a couple acres to a square mile, with small home ranges where food is abundant.

Description: Gliding membrane stretch from wrists to ankles; body fur soft, thi covers gliding membranes; tail flat latera Northern flying squirrel *(G. sabrinus)* sligh larger, often with red wash in fur; southe flying squirrel *(G. volans)* gray, sometimes w brown wash.

Size: Northern flying squirrel weight 4-5 o total length 10-11"; tail length 5"

Southern flying squirrel weight 2-3 oz.; to length 8-10"; tail length 3-4"

Range: Northern flying squirrel acro boreal forests of Canada to Alas south through western mou tains, to Great Lakes, a to north Atlantic US sta Southern flying squir throughout eastern US.

Minn.

Wisc.

Mich.

Northern Flying Squirrel
Glaucomys sabrinus

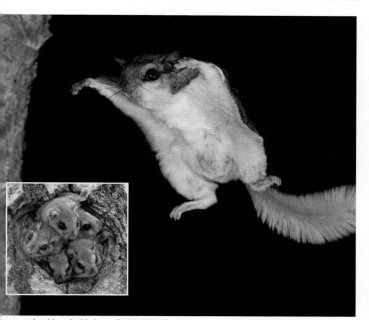

se guys should probably be called "gliding" squirrels as they don't fly but glide from tree ee via their "parachutes," flaps of skin connecting rear legs and fore legs. Inset: Flying rels may communally roost in old woodpecker holes nest boxes and other tree cavities.

od: Herbivore to omnivore: seeds of conifer and broad-leaved trees, buds, catkins, insects, birds and eggs. Northern flying squirrel diet ost entirely mushrooms and other fungal parts in many areas of range. thern flying squirrel depends more on seeds, less on fungi.

tural History: Both squirrels fall prey to diverse, nocturnal, avian mammalian predators. Young of both are born in a tree cavity in late ng after a 5-6 week gestation. Litter size is usually 2-4 naked young eyes and ears closed. Weaning occurs around 6 weeks of age but ngsters may stay with their mothers for some time afterward.

havior: Nocturnal with activity peaks after dusk and before dawn. y travel on the ground as well as glide between trees. Glides are usu- less than 25 yards.

wing Tips: Come to bird lers at night. Sometimes be heard running across a f. If a tree has an obvious ty over 10 feet from the nd, try knocking on the during the day. A flying rrel might peer out.

Southern Flying Squirrel
Glaucomys volans

Arctic Shrew *Sorex arcticus*

Highest populations in marshes and grassy clearings; spruce-tamarack bog

Nature Notes:

Density may reach 2-4 per acre. Breeding season begins in February in Wisconsin, later further north. Several litters of 5-9 can be produced each season. Eighty percent of Arctic shrews die before reaching sexual maturity.

Arctic shrews are active day and night, alternating foraging with resting.

Other Names: black-backed shrew, sadd back shrew.

Description: Distinctive tricolor coat w dark brown to black back, lighter brown dark golden sides, gray belly; tail indistinc bicolored.

Size: Weight ¼-½ oz.; total length 4-5"; length 1½-1¾"

Range: Great Lakes northwest to the Yuk and northeast to the St. Lawrence Seaw also in Nova Scotia but not Michigan's Lo Peninsula.

Food: Insectivore: insects, other in tebrates.

Minn.

Wisc.

Mich.

Common (Masked) Shrew *Sorex cinereus*

habitats, from dense forest to shrub lands to grasslands.

Other Names: masked shrew, cinereus shrew

Description: Nondescript; body uniformly brown; tail with blackish tip and greater than % of total length.

Size: Weight ¼ oz.; total length 3-5"; tail length 1-2"

Range: From tundra in Alaska and Canada to northeast US, to south of the Great Lakes and the southern Rocky Mountains.

Food: Insectivore: insects, other invertebrates.

Natural History: Common shrews breed from spring through autumn, litter size 4-10. Young are born hairless with eyes and ears closed and are weaned when about 3 weeks old, shortly after eyes open.

Nature Notes:

Our most common shrew.

Common shrews are somewhat more active at night than during the day, alternating foraging with resting.

Smoky Shrew   *Sorex fumeus*

Moist forest.

Nature Notes:

A smoke-colored shrew.

Smoky shrews twitter while foraging; this twittering may be echolocation.

Smoky shrews are somewhat more active at night than during the day, alternating foraging with resting.

Considered "Threatened" in Michigan, and "Special Concern" in Minnesota.

Description: Body gray to gray-brown summer; gray in winter; young are gray th first summer.

Size: Weight ¼-½ oz.; total length 4-5"; length 1½-2"

Range: From north of Lake Superior to N Scotia and south along the Appalachians.

Food: Insectivore: insects, other invertebrat

Natural History: Smoky shrews do not br during their first year but produce 2-3 ters of 3-7 young dur their second spring and e summer. Young stay v their mothers until ne full grown. Most females after reproduction.

Minn.

Wisc.

Mich.

gmy Shrew   *Sorex hoyi*

habitats of the North Woods.

scription: Small, nondescript; body brown; often obscured in fur; tail less than 40% of l length.

e: Weight ¼ oz.; total length 2-4"; tail ,th 1½-2"

ige: From the boreal forests of Alaska and ada south just into the US except in the at Plains.

d: Insectivore: insects, other invertebrates.

:ural History: Breeding probably from ng into autumn, litter size 2-8.

Nature Notes:

Our smallest shrew.

Pygmy shrews are active day and night, alternating foraging with resting.

Minn.

Wisc.

Mich.

American Water Shrew *Sorex palustris*

Most habitats near water.

Nature Notes:

The shrew that swims.

Water shrews forage in water (photo above) and also dive into water to avoid predators.

Predators include predatory fish, garter snakes, and terrestrial mammalian and avian predators.

Other Names: northern water shrew

Description: Large long-tailed shrew; bo black, sometimes frosted gray, never brov feet with stiff hairs fringing toes.

Size: Weight ½-1 oz.; total length 5-7"; length 2-3"

Range: Apparent disjunct range: from sou east Alaska south to central Rocky Mountai from west-central Canada southeast to Great Lakes, then northeast to Labrador, N Scotia and Maine.

Food: Insectivore: diverse insect larvae adult aquatic insects, even small fish. In restrial habitats, insects, invertebra

Natural History: Breed fr spring into autumn, prod ing probably 2-3 litters of young. They do not rep duce during the year t are born.

Minn.

Wisc.

Mich.

orthern Short-tailed Shrew *Blarina brevicauda*

bitats with dense ground cover.

er Names: mole shrew

scription: Big shrew the size of a deer use but with a typical, pointed shrew muz- body uniform gray or silver; tail short.

e: Weight ¾-1 oz.; total length 4-6"; tail ₃th 1-1¼"

ıge: From central to north-central Great ns east through the central-Atlantic US es north to Nova Scotia.

od: Insectivore: sometimes small vertebrates uding mice and voles.

ural History: Females n deliver two litters of young, one in spring, other in late summer. vborns are the size of a ey bee, naked with closed and eyes. Young are ned at 3½ weeks and can d by 7 weeks.

Nature Notes:

Short-tailed shrews can be quite noisy as they forage under leaf litter. They use high clicks to navigate by echolocation. Their saliva is venomous, is chewed into prey, and helps subdue small mammals and big invertebrates.

Short-tailed shrews forage under the leaf litter and in trenches and shallow holes in the ground.

Eastern Mole *Scalopus aquaticus*

Habitats with moist, loamy or sandy soils.

Nature Notes:

We once found one in the stomach of a northern pike, proving that eastern moles sometimes forage under water, as do star-nosed moles.

A mole may eat ⅓ of its body weight in invertebrates each day. Dirt removed from tunnels is piled above ground or used to fill shallow foraging tunnels.

Description: Black to gray; eyes minusc... no external ear pinnae; tail hairless.

Size: Weight 2-5 oz.; total length 5-8"; length ½-1"

Range: Eastern US except north-Atlantic sta...

Food: Insectivore: insects, other invertebrat...

Natural History: Spend 99% of their li... underground in their tunnels; two types: d... permanent tunnels and shallow warm-sea... ones. Populations cycle with the populati... of periodical cicadas (a.k.a. "17-year locust... Mole populations grow as cicada nym... grow bigger and bigger each year un... ground. After the cicada m... emergence, mole numb... crash, only to rebuild over... next 13 or 17 years.

Minn.

Wisc.

Mich.

ar-nosed Mole *Condylura cristata*

bitats with moist soils.

scription: Unmistakable; 22 fleshy, finger-appendages around its nostrils; guard hairs no nap; eyes minuscule; no external ear ae; tail hairless.

e: Weight 1½-3 oz.; total length 6-9"; tail th 2-4"

ge: Range forms a triangle from the itoba-US border northeast to the southeast ador coast to the Georgia coast, and back.

d: Insectivore: insects, aquatic crustaceans, r invertebrates, small fish.

ural History: Breed once ar; litter of 3-7 young in spring; newborns naked grow rapidly and become pendent by 3-4 weeks of Natal nests lined with leaves and grass, and located under root es or fallen trees.

Nature Notes:

Nose appendages are sensitive to touch and to electric fields of aquatic prey; can also manipulate prey.

Forage day and night and are more likely than other moles to forage above ground, especially at night. Sometimes forage in water.

Deposit fat in their tails before the breeding season.

Look for hump-topped foraging tunnels.

Minn.

Wisc.

Mich.

Former Resident

Bison *Bison bison*

Other Names: buffalo, North American buffalo

Order Cetartiodactyla—Even-toes hooved mammals and whales. Family Bovidae, cow and antelope family; bison, cattle, African and Asian antelope, sheep, goats.

Description: Not easily mistaken for any other mammal. Huge cow-like mammal with distinct hump above its shoulders and big head car ried low; body brown to black.

Range: Formerly across much of North America from the Great Plains, west to grasslands in Washington and Oregon, east through ea ern forests as far north as New York and south to the Gulf of Mexico The range extended into eastern Minnesota and central Wisconsin.

Fringe Species

Western Harvest Mouse *Reithrodontomys megalotis*

How you will recognize it: A small, pretty mouse. Body brown wi tan highlights. Belly white. Tail hairy, brown above, white below. De mouse and white-footed mouse distinctly larger with larger ears and eyes. Most house mice larger, more gray than brown, and house mice have mostly naked, gray tails not bicolored.

Where you might see it: Eastern Minnesota and west-central Wisconsin in prairies, meadows and overgrown pastures.

Prairie Vole *Microtus ochrogaster*

How you will recognize it: Body brown. Belly gray with yellow- t rusty-tipped fur. Tail medium length for a vole. Meadow vole usuall bigger, has finer body hair, gray belly and longer tail. Pine (woodlan vole is usually smaller, has much finer fur, very small eyes and ears, shorter tail. Southern bog lemming is usually smaller, body fur brow but mixed with black and silver, belly silver, upper incisors with long tudinal groove down the front.

Where you might see it: Eastern Minnesota and west-central Wisconsin in prairies, meadows and overgrown pastures.

Northern bog lemming *Synaptomys borealis*

How you will recognize it: Like southern bog lemming but with buff patches under ears.

Where you might see it: NW MN or Ontario north of Lk. Supe

lains Pocket Mouse *Perognathus flavescens*

ow you will recognize it: Small, golden to brown mouse. Belly
ite. Hind feet relatively large. Deer mouse and white-footed mouse
ger with larger ears and eyes; these mice have bicolored tails with
ite underside while pocket mouse has yellow underside Most house
ce larger, more gray or brown; house mice have mostly naked, gray
s not bicolored and not yellow.

ere you might see it: Eastern Minnesota in sand dunes and areas
h sandy soils.

lains Pocket Gopher *Geomys bursarius*

w you will recognize it: Body about 6 inches long with tail about
f its body length, light brown to brown to black. Eyes and ears small
visible. Forefeet with long claws. Incisors protruding, often visible.
les have distinctly pointed faces while gopher muzzle is more blunt,
les' eyes and ears not visible, and moles' forepaws broad and flat also
h long, sturdy claws.

ere you might see it: Eastern Minnesota and western Wisconsin
grassland with sandy to loamy soils, roadsides, pastures, golf courses.
dom above ground but distinctive mounds of soil, removed from
nel systems, seen in grassy areas.

iry-tailed Mole *Parascalops breweri*

w you will recognize it: Body about 5 inches long, brown to gray
lack. Tail short, hairy. Muzzle comes to distinct point. Forefeet very
, broad, with large claws. Eastern mole does not have a hairy tail
its range does not extend far north of Lake Erie. Star-nosed mole
distinctive star-shaped nose.

ere you might see it: East and north of Lake Huron in most
tats from forest to grassland with light soils.

ast Shrew *Cryptotis parva*

v you will recognize it: Very small shrew. Body brown in sum-
, gray in winter. Tail short, less than half the head and body length.
g-tailed shrews are mostly larger and have distinctly longer tails.
thern short-tailed shrew distinctly bigger, often mouse-sized, more
.

ere you might see it: Southern Wisconsin and the southern
nt of Michigan's Lower Peninsula in grassy, weedy, brushy fields.

Glossary

Alpha: First letter in the Greek alphabet, often used to designate t
dominant or parent individual of each sex in a wolf pack or coyote pa

Antlers: The paired, bony structures on the heads of members of
the deer family. Antlers are shed each winter and regrow each spring
through summer.

Aquatic: Living in water or having to do with water.

Binocular vision: Having both eyes aimed forward enough so that
areas visible by the 2 eyes overlap, allowing an animal to see clearly in
dimensions.

Bipedal: Walking on 2 legs; usually meaning the 2 hind legs but son
times meaning the 2 forelegs.

Blastocyst: A fetus at the stage of development that is a ball of cells
ready to implant in the uterine wall. This stage usually occurs appro:
mately 1-2 weeks after fertilization.

Cache: Food or another critical resource hidden for later retrieval and

Caecum (plural caeca): A sac attached to the large intestine just p
the point where the large intestine begins and the small intestine end
The caecum houses bacteria that digest the cell walls of plants, releas
the nutrients within those cells for a mammal to digest.

Cambium: The inner, living layer of bark on a tree. Nutrients produced in leaves flow through the cambium to the roots.

Canine teeth: In most mammals, large, pointed teeth located behir
the incisors and before the cheek teeth (premolars and molars). Som
mammals, such as rodents and rabbits, lack canine teeth. In deer, lov
canine teeth masquerade as incisors.

Carnassial teeth: The last upper premolar and first lower molar o
each side of the mouth of carnivores (members of the Order Carnivc
These teeth are shaped to be able to shear skin, muscles, tendons, or
meat and other body parts of vertebrates. They are self-sharpening.

Carnivore: An animal that eats other vertebrates as its main food
source. Also, a common name for mammals in the Order Carnivora
of whom have other vertebrates as a main source of food or who hav
evolved from mammals that do. The Order Carnivora is defined as
including only those mammals with carnassial teeth or having evolve
from mammals who had them.

nivorous: Having a diet composed mostly of vertebrate animals.

rion: Dead body parts of vertebrates.

tor: The sweet smelling discharge from the castor glands of bea-
. Used by beavers to mark their territories. Often used by humans
ie manufacture of perfumes to hold scents.

atonic: A condition of not being able to move.

ity: A hole in a tree or hole in the ground.

ek teeth: A name for premolars and molars considered together.

onial roost: A resting site where many flying animals aggregate.
ally used for birds and bats.

nmensal: Being dependent on members of another species for
ortant resources, such as food and shelter, while not affecting the
of members of those other species.

rophagy: Eating feces. Although not literally accurate, also refers
ie eating of partly digested plant material that has been made
stible by bacteria living in a mammal's caecum and that is extruded
mass from the anus.

ptic: Having coloration and habitats by which an animal blends
the background environment.

p: The rounded or sharp point of a tooth.

iduous teeth: Baby teeth; the first teeth that most mammals get
n they are young and which are shed during the process of growing
t teeth.

ecation: The passing of solid waste from the anus.

ayed implantation: Having a period in early pregnancy when a
loping fetus in the blastocyst stage goes dormant and ceases devel-
ent for days to months instead of implanting in the uterine wall.

: A site, usually a tree cavity, hollow log or hole in the ground, in
h a mother mammal cares for her offspring. Mothers give birth in
l dens and use maternal dens to care for young. Also a site where a
imal, such as a bear, raccoon or skunk, that is inactive during win-
ays.

tal formula: An efficient presentation for the numbers of incisor, canine, premolar and molar teeth that a mammal has in each quadrant of its mouth.

Dentary: The bone on each side of the jaw of a mammal.

Dentine: Hard tissue filling most of the interior of mammal teeth inside the enamel.

Diastema: The large space between the incisors and the cheek teeth many herbivorous mammals, notably rodents and terrestrial cetartiodact

Digit: A finger or toe, including thumb and big toe.

Diurnal: Being active during daylight hours.

Diversity: Having many different kinds of members within a group. In an ecological context, diversity often refers to having members of many different species living in a place.

DNA: Abbreviation for deoxyribonucleic acid, which is the molecule that contains genes.

Dominate: Referring to an individual animal: to direct the behavior of other members of its social group, such as displacing other membe of the group to obtain food. An animal that dominates is dominant.

Dormant: When an organism slows the processes of life to the poin that life almost appears suspended.

Ear pinna (plural pinnae): The external ear, that part of an ear tha sticks out from the head.

Echolocation: The process of sending sounds, hearing the parts of those sounds that bounce back, and processing the returning sounds understand the environment.

Enamel: The hard outer covering of the teeth of most mammals.

Epizootic: Among animals, an outbreak of disease that affects many animals at once. The equivalent of an epidemic in humans.

Evolution: The process of changing gene frequencies within a popu-tion. The process by which the proportion of individuals in a popula-tion having a particular trait changes.

Exfoliate: To remove the layers of something.

Extirpate: Causing a species to go extinct, usually considered to be action of humans.

Feral: Describing a domestic animal that lives in the wild, indepen of humans.

dock: The external nubbin of a rudimentary toe on hooved mammals that has reduced in size through evolution, usually covered with ugh skin and elevated above the toes that touch the ground.

us: The developing offspring of a mammal during gestation.

age: To look for something; for mammals, usually, to look for food.

gmentation: The state of having been cut or divided into pieces.

givorous: Having a diet composed mostly of fruit.

eralized body build: The body shape of a mammal that walks legs; has forelegs, hind legs and back of roughly equal length; has 5 on each foot; has a tail; and a neck a bit longer than its head.

etics: The study of inheritance.

us: The first word in the scientific name of an organism. For mple, *Canis*, in *Canis lupus*, the scientific name for wolves.

tation: The period of the development of fetal mammals lasting when the blastocyst implants in the uterus until birth.

dle: To remove the bark, including the inner bark, all the way id a tree so that no nutrients can flow down the tree to its roots. lling a tree kills the tree.

nds: A group of specialized cells that work together to make and crete a substance. Glands within a mammal's digestive system help st food. Some glands on a mammal's skin secrete substances used to municate with other mammals.

rd hair: The tough, outer hairs on a mammal that protect its insu-g underfur and skin.

itat: The vegetative and physical environment around an organ-that provides resources that the organism needs, such as food and ter.

ituate: To become accustomed to or to cause another animals to me accustomed to.

bivorous: Having a diet composed mostly of diverse vegetation.

ernate: For a mammal or bird to enter a sleeplike state by lowering hetabolic rate and reducing its body temperature to slightly above temperature of its surroundings for an extended period, usually for t of winter, and thereby reducing food and water requirements. ernation requires an extended time for arousal.

Home range: The area where an animal lives, where it is familiar with resources, knows where to find food and water, and knows how escape from predators.

Hoof: The horny covering on the tips of the toes of deer, antelopes horses on which they walk; the equivalent of an enlarged fingernail or cl

Horns: The paired projections on the heads of antelopes, sheep and goats. Horns have a core of bone and have a tough cover.

Hybridize: To produce offspring from breeding with a member of different species.

Implantation: In mammalian reproduction, the action of a blastocy imbedding within the uterine wall of its mother and beginning to p duce a placenta.

Incisor teeth: The front teeth in a mammal's mouth, generally use to manipulate food. Most are small but the incisors of rodents, rabb and hares are large and are used to slice vegetation.

Infrared radiation: Waves of light just beyond the wavelengths of light that humans can see.

Insectivorous: Having a diet composed mostly of insects and, usu other invertebrate animals.

Invertebrate: An animal without a backbone.

Juvenile: An immature organism.

Lactate: To produce milk in mammary glands as food for offspring

Lateral: Referring to the sides.

Leaf litter: The layer of leaves and other plant parts that lies on top the soil.

Leveret: A baby rabbit, hare or pica.

Longitudinal groove: On mammalian teeth, an indentation that r along the outfacing surface of a tooth from the tip to the gum.

Mammary glands: The glands of mammals that produce milk for offspring to drink.

Marsupial: A mammal in the major group of mammals, the Marsupia that are highly specialized to support their offspring with milk and t have rudimentary placentas and very short gestation periods.

Maternal colony: A group of female mammals all of whom are rai offspring.

aternal den: A site, usually a tree cavity or hollow log or hole in the
ound, in which a mother mammal raises her offspring.

atriarch: An old and dominant female who usually has an important
e in deciding what a group of related females will do and where they
Il go.

embrane: A thin tissue within a body.

ercaptans: Sulphur compounds; in mammals these are the sulphur
mpounds made in anal glands and other glands and used for com-
inication with other mammals. Also the sulphur compounds used by
inks for defense.

etabolism: The chemical activity and reactions within an organism's
dy that sustain its life.

dden: The collective food cache of a squirrel.

grate: To make a repeated and predictable movement across a land-
pe, during specific times of year.

olar teeth: The farthest-back teeth in a mammal's mouth.

olt: In mammals, to shed old hair and grow new hair.

ip: Related to animal hair, hair lying in a direction and not straight up.

tal colony: A group of females all of whom are giving birth, about
give birth, or have just given birth.

tal den: A site, usually a tree cavity or hollow log or hole in the
ound, in which a mother mammal gives birth.

onate: A newborn mammal.

octurnal: Being active during night-time hours.

otochord: The cartilaginous-like rod that lies from head to tail in
ordates. Animals that have notochords at some period of their devel-
ment are grouped in the Phylum Chordata and are called chordates.
vertebrates the notochord becomes boney during development.

xious: Repulsive, poisonous or dangerous.

nnivorous: Having a diet composed of both plant and animal matter.

ulate: For a mammal to shed an egg, or ovum, from its ovary.

ir bond: A close relationship between a female and male animal,
ually related to mating.

Palmate: Shaped like the palm of a hand.

Pedicel: The boney protrusion on the top of a deer's head from whi[ch] an antler grows.

Placenta: The organ connecting a fetus to its mother while the fetus [is] within its mother's uterus. The placenta provides the fetus with nutrients and removes waste materials.

Precocial: Capable of a high degree of independent activity from bir[th].

Predator: An animal that kills and eats other animals.

Prehensile: Adapted for gripping or manipulating.

Premolar teeth: The teeth behind the canines and in front of the molars in most mammals' mouths.

Quadrant: Related to mammal teeth, a quarter of a mammal's mout[h], upper left side, lower left side, upper right side, lower right side.

Quill: A very stiff, sharp, pointed guard hair having pointed scales tha[t] make it rough when rubbed shaft to tip but smooth when rubbed tip to shaft. A quill pulls easily from its follicle so that it can stick into a predator.

Rabies: A deadly viral disease of mammals and birds that causes acu[te] inflammation in the brain, that may cause the animal to behave errati[]cally, and that is fatal in humans.

Raptor: A predatory bird, a hawk or an owl.

Regurgitate: To bring food materials that have been swallowed bac[k] up the esophagus and into the mouth.

Rendezvous site: Related to wolves, where a wolf pack congregate[s] for a period of days or weeks when pups are not yet able to forage an[d] hunt with the adults.

Resident: An organism that lives in a specific place.

Resource: A material that is needed for life, such as food and shelte[r].

Rudimentary: Primitive or not fully developed.

Rumen: In ruminant mammals, the first of 3 sacs at the end of the esophagus and before the stomach. Bacteria in the rumen digest the c[el]lulose in the cell walls of the vegetation that the mammal swallows.

Ruminant: A mammal that has a rumen; specifically a mammal with a set of families, including the deer Family, or the Cervidae, within th[e] Order Cetartiodactyle.

or Young Readers

y, William D. 1988. *Deneki: An Alaskan Moose.* Press North America.

s, Mary. 2007. *Wolf Song.* Raven Productions, Inc.

kford, Cheryl. 2015. *Hungry Coyote.* Minnesota Historical Society
s.

en, Betsy. (1993) 2015. *Tracks in the Wild.* University of Minnesota
s.

son-Voiles, Polly. 2008. *Someone Walks By: The Wonders of Winter
dlife.* Raven Productions, Inc.

gonwagon, Crescent. 1997. *Bat in the Dining Room.* Marshall Caven-
.

ng, Susan. 1996. *Lucky Hares and Itchy Bears.* Alaska Northwest
ks.

nerstron, Frances. (1975) 2013. *Walk When the Moon Is Full.* R.
neider, Publishers.

s, Jennifer Berry. 2001. *Who Lives in the Snow?* Roberts Rinehart.

ens, Mary Beth. 1988. *A Caribou Alphabet.* The Dog Ear Press.

ell, Consie. (1995) 2007. *A Bold Carnivore: An Alphabet of Predators.*
en Productions, Inc.

s, Michael Elsohn. 2007. *Mama's Milk.* Tricycle Press.

nan, Joyce. 2010. *Dark Emperor & Other Poems of the Night.* Hough-
Mifflin Books for Children.

nan, Joyce. 2010. *Ubiquitous: Celebrating Nature's Survivors.* Hough-
Mifflin Books for Children.

nan, Joyce. 2014. *Winter Bees & Other Poems of the Cold.* Houghton
flin Harcourt.

Index

Great Northern Naturalist *Homo curiosus*

adult ♂

All habitats from dense forest to prairie, desert, farm land and urban areas.

Nature Notes:

Order: Primata; monkeys, apes and other fools. Family: Hominidae; butchers, bakers, candlestick makers.

Most monkeys and apes are tropical in distribution in Africa, Asia and South America. Only the Naturalist has a world-wide distribution. Primates fall into 4 groups: lemurs and lorises, New World monkeys, Old World monkeys and apes. Most are predominantly herbivorous or omnivorous, eating fruits, nuts, some leaves, insects and some tubers. Some species do prey on other vertebrates at times. Almost all primates have 2 incisors in each quadrant of the mouth, 1 canine, and variable numbers of cheek teeth, which have low, rounded cusps for crushing and grinding their varied foods

Highly variable with contradictive behaviors

Other Names: treehugger, birdwatcher, bird herper, bugwatcher, tree worshiper, nature nu

Size: male 5'3"-6'6"; female 4'10"-6'0"; t absent; weight: 90-250+ lbs.

Description: Large, highly variable, usua bipedal mammal; body covering highly va able, in summer body covering woven or kr in winter body covering sometimes thick a fuzzy or fluffy. Four morphs in North Wooc

1) *Upwatcher.* This morph wanders, usu: looking up, often through eye-extension piec It appears inordinately fixated on birds a makes sudden movements accompanied by v ied exclamatory sounds that may be very lc or very soft: *t-h-i-s-w-a-a-a-y-y-y-y*, or *ooooc* or *ahhhhhh*, or **$&^*!#$!*

2) *Downwatcher.* This morph wanders, usu: looking down. It frequently stops to turn o logs or to look under rocks. It can be noctum

herd

adult ♀

juvenile
(in the wild)

ecially on warm, drizzly nights, when it crawls for hours on its hands
knees. It is quick and able to catch small vertebrates.

Clicker. This morph carries a fist-sized box strapped to its chest or
ging from its neck. Often, it stops to look through the box, some-
es kneeling and holding the box very close to objects, other times
ding and pointing the box across open landscapes. When the box
kes an audible click, this morph often returns to wandering.

Speeder. Always travels in a large metal box of variable color at speeds
er than any mammal can run. It stops at scenic places but usually
/s inside its large box. Occasionally it gets out of the box and walks
edally to a place with a good view and might pause, almost always
less than a minute. Then it returns to its large box and speeds away.
casionally when it stops, it transforms briefly into a Clicker.

od: Highly variable. Some completely herbivorous. Others carnivo-
s, though most carnivorous Naturalists do not kill prey but scavenge.
st Naturalists appear omnivorous.

tural History: Home range large. Predators unknown, though any
nber of medium-sized, mammalian predators should be able to kill
eat them. Why predation has not been observed is a major question.
production must be prodigious because populations of these mammals
w at exponential rates.

ewing Tips: Go to any natural area and observe. You do not even
d a blind to watch members of this species because they are usually
ivious to anything not related to a days' objectives.

Other user-friendly field guides from Kollath-Stensaas Publishing

Fascinating Fungi of the North Woods
Cora Mollen & Larry Weber

Wildflowers of the BWCA & North Shore
Mark Sparky Stensaas

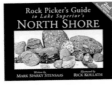

Rock Picker's Guide to Lake Superior's North Shore
Mark Sparky Stensaas

Amazing Agates: Lake Superior's Banded Gemstone
Scott Wolter

Orchids of the North Woods

Kim & Cindy Risen

Ferns of the North Woods

Joe Walewski

Insects of the North Woods

Jeff Hahn

Moths of the North Woods

Jim Sogaard

Dragonflies of the North Woods

Kurt Mead

Lichens of the North Woods

Joe Walewski

Spiders of the North Woods

Larry Weber

Butterflies of the North Woods

Larry Weber